on track short ...

MC5

every album, every song

Richard Butterworth

sonicbondpublishing.com

Sonicbond Publishing Limited
www.sonicbondpublishing.co.uk
Email: info@sonicbondpublishing.co.uk

First Published in the United Kingdom 2026
First Published in the United States 2026

British Library Cataloguing in Publication Data:
A Catalogue record for this book is available from the British Library

Typeset in ITC Garamond Std & ITC Avant Garde Gothic
Printed and bound in England

Graphic design and typesetting: Full Moon Media

on track short ...

MC5

every album, every song

Richard Butterworth

sonicbondpublishing.com

For Sue, for ever

Foreword: mea culpas, etc

Welcome to MC5 101, from foundation in 1963 to termination just under a decade later. Meaning no disrespect to the careers of young musicians still learning to walk upright when MC5 fell, I've illuminated their subsequent activities only with the broadest of brushes. This means a hard pass on numerous post-5 solo albums and some middling to fine rock groups, such as Ascension, Gang War, Destroy All Monsters and the incendiary Sonic's Rendezvous Band. I've instead focused on MC5's colourful Detroit backstory, the rise of hardass Motor City rock and the musical stimuli that married Chuck Berry to Sun Ra, with The Who as best man. I've parsed the early singles and the albums *Kick Out The Jams*, *Back In The USA* and *High Time*, all set against the countercultural ferment of late 1960s America and MC5's much-misinterpreted socio-political posture. The latter informed the treacheries, well-meaning accidents and personal cockups that inhibited the band's progress as a rock 'n' roll force to be reckoned with – at least during their short lifetime, if not since as a pivotal influence on innumerable younger groups. I've concluded with brief summaries of the better bootlegs, some 'what MC5 did next' resumés and a digest of the final LP attributed to MC5, *Heavy Lifting*, released in 2024 and originally intended as the latest in a string of solo projects by the 5's leader, Wayne Kramer.

All of the appraisals and critiques are mine, based on knowledge, research and the sado-masochistic affection for MC5 I've retained since *Kick Out The Jams* first assaulted my reason in March 1969. Everyone has their own take on events occluded by sixty-odd years, fake news and clouds of reefer smoke, and I hope it goes without saying that your opinions of the 5, their music and their lasting impact are every inch as valid as mine. As for the facts, this history is only as accurate as the disparate and often highly conflicting source material allows. Again, you may differ. Perhaps you were getting on down to MC5 in the Grande Ballroom on Devil's Night, 1968. If so, I remain profoundly envious, my bad if I've got it all wrong and after you with the Rocket Reducer. Reheating in particular the chaotic stew of the band's last few months can only ever be subject to endless disputes and revisionism, and MC5 ain't telling: sadly they're all now passed on, as is manager and mentor, John Sinclair: a key influence on the band's development and – though not always welcomed by Brothers Wayne, Fred, Rob, Michael and Dennis – their notoriety. Forgive, too, my occasional licence for effect; there's definitely a Black Sabbath Bridge in Birmingham, but I can't be certain I've ever heard AC/DC playing in Tesco.

Would you like to write for Sonicbond Publishing?

At Sonicbond Publishing we are always on the look-out for authors, particularly for our two main series:

On Track. Mixing fact with in depth analysis, the On Track series examines the work of a particular musical artist or group. All genres are considered from easy listening and jazz to 60s soul to 90s pop, via rock and metal.

On Screen. This series looks at the world of film and television. Subjects considered include directors, actors and writers, as well as entire television and film series. As with the On Track series, we balance fact with analysis.

While professional writing experience would, of course, be an advantage the most important qualification is to have real enthusiasm and knowledge of your subject. First-time authors are welcomed, but the ability to write well in English is essential.

Sonicbond Publishing has distribution throughout Europe and North America, and all books are also published in E-book form. Authors will be paid a royalty based on sales of their book.

Further details are available from www.sonicbondpublishing.co.uk. To contact us, complete the contact form there or email info@sonicbondpublishing.co.uk

on track short ...
MC5

Contents

Introduction

Any colour the customer wants, as long as it's black.

It was an ironic aside, never a selling proposition. But Henry Ford's neat, ever-quotable motto from his 1922 memoir became forever hitched to Detroit's automobile industry: the waking behemoth that would ignite America's post-Depression economic recovery and spawn a global superpower. In the Motor City nearly half a century later, societal decline was already oxidising the juggernaut mobilised by Ford, William C. Durant and Ransome Olds when five young musicians, so ill-mannered they threatened truth, justice and the stock prices of a department store and two recording companies, bottled their own ideology with a pithy one-liner.

Well, kinda:

KICK OUT THE JAMS, MOTHERFUCKERS!

Rarely was Madison Avenue more concise, no adman's slogan more persistently misunderstood. At a time when such demands seemed to carry some weight, this felt like a super-militant call-to-action, a 'Your Country Needs You' for countercultural babyboomers. No one seemed sure who was kicking out whom. Was this a rallying cry to take to the streets and throw petrol bombs at police? Or a plea to ban the sale and non-recreational use of strawberry preserves? In fact, it was a handful of Motor City factory rats, souls bared and buzzing like unearthed circuitry, causing nearly every other rock group to quake in their snakeskin boots. Brothers and sisters, I give you a testimonial: The MC5.

MC5 were streetwise escapees from Detroit's auto assembly plants; the bluecollar, co-founding brethren of that imprecise symptom of cultural decline we know as punk. In the hardest of US smokestack towns, MC5 forged some of the toughest rock 'n' roll imaginable, generating energy that could light the Heartlands. MC5 knew no guardrails, happy only when scaring the bejazus out of straight and freak society alike. With the Summer of Love turned inside-out to bitter winter, MC5 took America's cultural establishment by its tatty, tie-dyed kaftan and shook till the rest of the colours ran. Barely out of their teens, MC5's swaggering air of superiority and entitlement was born of the certainty they did rock 'n' roll better than almost everyone, and of the entirely plausible expectancy that, pretty soon, the rest would be left gasping.

And MC5 (definite article optional) rarely hesitated to let any pretender who dared share their limelight know it. Bellowed from the wings of a theatre – usually Detroit's stately, crumbly Grande Ballroom, the 5's home turf – 'kick out the jams' (motherfuckers optional) was the sound of MC5 marking their territory, cocking their legs over reputations they felt – they knew – were barely deserved. Any group, supporting or headline, thought to be merely 'jamming' and thereby bilking a paying audience was heckled mercilessly. 'We harassed every band we played with,' guitarist and leader Wayne Kramer explained to *Uncut*. 'If they were losers, we let them know.

We'd stand by the edge of the stage and holler: 'Kick out the jams or get off the stage!'

The potential humiliation of following this combustible music while the amps were still hot was coveted by few. Blue Cheer, one evening's scheduled bill-toppers and, at the time, the group routinely touted as the world's loudest, sensibly declined. Blood, Sweat & Tears were expressly forbidden by their record company minders. Detroit deejay and MC5 associate Jerry Goodwin told of how Big Brother & The Holding Company refused to take the stage after the 5 played 'a blistering set ... I think [Janis Joplin's] words were, no fucking way.' Even Cream, on a good night a tough act to follow, received a red card.

A second coinage needed no decoding. Distilled to their essential salts, the words would become an enduring refrain, famously summarising an entire pop psychogeography, even titling a hit for Ian Dury. 'Total Assault on the culture through Rock 'n' roll, Dope and Fucking in the Streets' was the long version, Clause 2 of a fanciful political 'manifesto' concocted by John Sinclair: poet, journalist, founder of Detroit-based revolutionary activists Trans-Love Energies and the White Panther Party, disc jockey, free jazz fan, marijuana evangelist – and MC5's sometime manager, rabbi and huckster-in-chief.

With and without the charismatic Sinclair, MC5 scorched fiercely but briefly, releasing just three albums between 1969 and 1971 before the afterburners flared out a year later. Their natural feeding ground was the stage: scarier than a NORAD general on crystal meth, MC5 blasted off nightly to Alpha Centauri or Armageddon, whichever was further out. Lead vocalist Rob Tyner's moves lacked the animal grace of a Daltrey, Jagger or Morrison, still less such 5 heroes as James Brown or Otis Redding. Yet as he jumped, twisted and writhed with spasmodic abandon, all satin threads and whitebread 'fro, Tyner could have an audience in his palm within five minutes. Kramer and co-axeman Fred 'Sonic' Smith, guitars locked and loaded like duelling Kalashnikovs, skated giddily around the singer as if choreographed by Timothy Leary, lying prostrate or leaping onto speaker cabinets, discharging feedback-soaked solos that scraped at the eardrums like fingernails on chalkboard. His instruments' back skins removed for maximum volume, Dennis 'Machine Gun' Thompson's drumming was relentless; performing, as *Rolling Stone* enthused, 'with such intensity ... he must have the equipment man wipe the sweat off him while playing'. Only bassist Michael Davis was relatively impassive, trying, as he wrote in his memoir, 'to appear as cool and unconcerned as possible.' Instead of keeping the lid on the pressure cooker with Wymanesque detachment, however, Mike's playing was as loose and feverish as all the rest.

Between 1968 and 1969, the 5 took a raincheck from rock 'n' roll's approved wardrobe of black biker leather and faded blue denim. They'd parade onto a stage displaying gaudy showbiz threads run up on sewing machines by Trans-Love's 'old ladies'; spangly tat that glamrock's glittery hipsters would one day consider a uniform. The painted-on stars'n'bars pants and flouncy silk blousons were as ironic as the US flags draped over their backline. For despite the beefy music, and a buccaneering hardman demeanour that implied a shiv in every back pocket, MC5 knew they were, above all, entertainers.

As for their commitment to the era's faux-seditionary distractions, this would prove more stage-dressing than Total Assault. For a group so wedded to creative amplified mayhem, their declamatory messaging was never as shrill as John Sinclair's. MC5's 1969 live debut album nonetheless remained the sound of youth so heated Middle America cowered behind its screen door with a fire hose. As *Kick Out The Jams* demonstrated, this was no ordinary hard rock band. MC5 pulled off the three-card trick of folding into already dislocated cosmic blues and garage rock the torrid astringency of avant-garde jazz. They learned well on giants' shoulders, even occasionally sharing a stage with the legendary pianist, big-band leader and Afrofuturist, Sun Ra. A song might begin with a simple riff, straying no farther than two chords before self-destructing fifteen minutes later as a ruined cathedral of noise. Neither MC5's truculent rustbelt soul brothers, The Stooges, nor New York City's terrifying avant-punks The Velvet Underground – the balance of the American East Coast's troika of 1960s rock 'n' roll malpractice – were this brutal.

MC5 yanked most eagerly at the thread trailed by the early to mid-1960s British Invasion groups: The Rolling Stones, The Yardbirds, The Kinks, The Beatles. Of all the limey imports arousing America from its asexual, post-Elvis coma, the 5's most culpable influencers were The Who, the west London mods then marching steadily from sharp tailoring and Moe Howard hairdos towards boiler suits and rock-god corkscrew curls. In 1965, The Who's second single, 'Anyway, Anyhow, Anywhere', featured one of mainstream pop's earliest passages of guitar feedback, Pete Townshend's demented solo crashing the VU meter and guiding the adolescent fingers of Kramer and Smith as surely as ten pages of blues tabs. Trashing a good month's earnings at the 1967 Monterey Pop Festival, The Who presaged hippiedom's dark slide from gentle idealism, the unrestrained bombast of their show suggesting the flower-power memo was lost in transit. With the release of the peerless 'I Can See For Miles', whose timber-splintering riff and unhinged drumming eclipsed everything deemed proto-metal since 'You Really Got Me', The Who's impact on MC5 became unequivocal.

1970's *Live At Leeds* would remind everyone (including MC5) who'd actually invented this stuff. But Townshend's 1969 concept piece, *Tommy*, lent The Who a more intellectual heft than singer Roger Daltrey, at least, thought entirely healthy for four pill-popping mods from the White City. As far as five pill-popping punks from the Motor City were concerned, Daltrey had the right idea: the respect of the smartass classes was neither wanted nor needed. Instead, MC5 poured Townshend's earliest teen torment into their own music like liquid propellant into a Titan II, storming around Midwest stages ill-built to withstand such massive incoming. Only these pillaging berserkers could match the Londoners' explosive instability. Everyone else just needed to stand the hell back.

The Punk Ecosystem

> Beethoven was a punk, Picasso was a punk, everyone of a new generation
> who rejected the voice of a previous generation could be described as a punk.
> Wayne Kramer, interviewed by Jim Kerr for *Q104.3*, 2018

The story of punk varies according to every cultural historian. Punk's perennial anger-dump is sometimes conflated with broader tropes and individuals: Dylan, Woody Guthrie, Jack Kerouac, Phil Ochs, Greenwich Village coffee-houses, Beat poets and bebop; the pop-cultural saga of Western socio-political dissent harking back to the fearless, desperate field hollers resounding across the Mississippi Delta of 1928. A 'punk' narrative specific to MC5, however, can be built on simpler foundations: chaos both manufactured and accidental, torn-up recording contracts and untoward police interest – not to mention very loud, heavy, confrontational electric rock music.

Importantly, the term predates the popularly accepted timelines. In 1976, Richard Hell of Television became the first musician of record to investigate the sartorial possibilities of safety pins and bondage pants. Less born than exhumed, punk's foetid spirit quickly reconstituted and gained traction as a social idea. In London, supervised by the shrewd Chelsea shopkeeper Malcolm McLaren, The Sex Pistols bolted Doctor Feelgood and The Ramones into nihilist anarchy and British punk became a thing. Though nothing really new, this was still dangerous, iconoclastic stuff. Suddenly copies of *Wind & Wuthering* and *Olias Of Sunhillow* were as rare as Johnny Rotten's dental records. While The Clash bled radical chic and posed as armed freedom fighters for the proletariat, Siouxsie & The Banshees deconstructed a twenty-minute 'Lord's Prayer' for the early faithful at the 100 Club. As Sham 69's inchoate discontent drowned out Millwall FC's on the soccer terraces, The Damned took the mick and accidentally invented gobbing. Good old teenage rage, right there, from the real deal to the ersatz. And it had been baked into rock 'n' roll since forever.

The Pistols were smart enough to acknowledge an earlier influence. Even McLaren would quietly admit the partial debt owed by his unruly proteges to a previous client, if not the real spadework completed long before. Take a curtsy, then, New York Dolls: trailer-trash porn queens, cranked to high heaven and dripping in costume bling, platform pumps and Goodwill chiffon; druggy, disreputable and doomed. But if the Stones didn't break a sweat, for at least one album the Dolls wrote great songs and could rock like a bitch, exerting extra gravitational pull on the asteroid hurtling towards the UK (in 1977, The Clash's brilliant first album would ring with the licentious clamour of 1973's *New York Dolls*). But the knowing trashiness dovetailed less with the manly business of fighting the power – the Dolls were too smacked out to fight a mild headcold – than with the ironic burlesque of glamrock. Any coherent antagonism they harboured towards the status quo was buried beneath a topsoil of self-medicated indifference and Revlon.

The apathy on which the Dolls slouched was actually birthed c1965 in the garages of middle America. Armed with cheap department-store guitars and squeaky Farfisa organs, adenoidal kids jerked off the two-chord tricks that would run through the polite suburbs like Thunderbird wine pissed up against gas station drainpipes. Although this thin, joyously simple music had angst snot-sneered all over it, parents had little cause for broader concern. The rebellion was more likely about kicking the dog than the doors of City Hall, still less the walls of the Citadel. As soon as the kids had gotten it all out of their systems, General Motors and IBM would be processing the job applications and Mom and Pop could breathe easy again.

That was the theory. But didn't you know there's a war on? As opposition mounted to the insanity of US misadventure in South-East Asia, the music produced by its youth became louder and angrier. By 1968, amid flower-power hangover, the Tet Offensive, the Paris *événements*, political assassinations and nationwide race riots, the gloves were off for those early punk bands who dodged the Vietnam draft or whose employment submissions were rejected.

With Elektra Records' renowned 1972 collection *Nuggets*, the writer and Patti Smith Group guitarist, Lenny Kaye, codified the early punk subculture by compiling a malodorous heap of torment and teenage lust that still managed to overlook MC5. Lenny was a fan, but by now the venom harboured towards the 5 by Elektra label boss Jac Holtzman – a powerful industry figure whose early patronage of MC5 had long evaporated – was 200% concentrated, as we shall see.

This was the world that spawned MC5, then: the bastard sons of Chuck Berry and a Chevrolet steam forge. Grownups should look away now.

Today's approval ratings for MC5 as punk prophets are sky-high and near universal. The earliest critics were sceptical, due partially to an infamous magazine article that appeared to dump unbiased reportage in favour of specially commissioned, if well-meaning hype. Accompanying a crouched, madly frizzed Rob Tyner decorating the cover of *Rolling Stone* in January 1969, Ohio college kid Eric Ehrmann extolled the 5 in an eyepoppingly purple five-page main feature. Perhaps the cub reporter had convinced a kindly editor his piece didn't read like an over-stimulated Trans-Love Energies press release, but John Sinclair, TLE leader and then-manager of MC5, later swore he'd never encountered worse journalism in his life. Meanwhile Wayne Kramer dismissed as fallacious the old saw, 'no such thing as bad publicity'. As he reminded Jim Kerr of New York radio station *Q104.3* in 2018, MC5 were now professional potheads with drug tolerances way beyond those of wide-eyed student hacks:

[Eric] had never smoked reefer before, but we smoked non-stop, morning till night. So he got high with us, and hung out for a couple days, and he went home and wrote this story that was like a cartoon adventure, where he was having trouble discerning what was real and what wasn't, what was put on and what was a joke, what was sarcasm, what was cynicism.

If the boy Eric had boiled his first commission to a barely-readable word purée ('total destroy experience'?) at least it whet appetites – this fifteen year old author's among them. The real heartburn would come three months later, in the same magazine, when Lester Bangs filleted his colleague's overstatements with a mess of his own. The patent was still pending on the caustic erudition that would famously inform Bangs' style; it was hard to tell whether the once and future king of gonzo rock journalism was attacking MC5 or obliquely harpooning his frothing young colleague, as he opined in his first published album review: '[MC5] came on like a bunch of 16 year old punks on a meth power trip'. (He intended no compliment, but by 1977 such words would have been deemed less scornful than downright adoring.) Bangs logged out of his character assassination by comparing his subjects with The Troggs, the cartoonish British quartet whose winningly brainless hit version of Chip Taylor's 'Wild Thing' hinted of a bumptiously punky ethic lurking in the Wiltshire hedgerows. This was further intimated by The Troggs' infamous, hilariously sweary studio tape; and, despite their singer excreting the sexual allure of a chubby schoolboy caught filching pies from a tuck shop, an enduring teenybopper appeal.

In 1971, Lester manned up and admitted he'd called it wrong, getting drunk with Wayne Kramer and, after seeing MC5 at Detroit's Frütcellar, declaring 'there is no better band anywhere' with the zeal of the convert. By then, it was too late. Recanted or not, Bangs' hatchet job would be indelibly associated with the felling of MC5, helped along by numerous misadventures: the impatience and duplicity of record company executives; the censure of a major retailer and two of America's most influential promoters; a manager too keen to shoehorn reluctant musicians into pursuing socio-political change as if by presidential fiat; the excesses of pranksters turning dissent into a series of jokes; a roughneck band as easy to tame as a nest of sidewinders; and, inevitably, the oceanic drug abuse.

Bangs wasn't the only garlanded hack to miss the point. Over the years, too many critics have defaulted to at best revisionist, at worst plain ignorant interpretations of rock history. Some dismissed MC5 as courtiers to much less extravagant talents who, like time-serving politicians holding out for undeserved peerages, never seemed to leave. In 1991's *England's Dreaming*, for the most part a standard text on Britpunk and its forerunners, Jon Savage sidelined MC5 with two brief sentences. He circled back in February 2024, in time to see MC5 finally pressed into the Rock and Roll Hall of Fame – an honour that surely would have prodded the original band, all by then sadly passed on, into starting the revolution straight away. Savage paid belated tribute to Kramer on social media and, tasked by *Britannica* to trace punk's lineage, finally gave MC5 their due, alongside The New York Dolls and Iggy & The Stooges.

At time of writing, Iggy Pop, hardworking and creative enough to keep himself in the public eye, his shows still formidable despite scoliosis and a bad hip scuppering the stage-diving, is routinely lauded as the artist who has wielded most authority over badass modern outlaw rock. It's not this writer's intention to belittle the talent and impact of the Godfather of Punk; even if the latter accolade is debatable, some of Iggy's albums, with and without The Stooges, stand up among the hottest of the past half century. But it is only right that, as of today, MC5 are acclaimed the true pioneers of that nebulous phenomenon; indeed, of most popular music, irrespective of genre or media construct, threatening to bring down societal rafters without worrying too much about what dodgy totalitarian building firm might succeed them.

Whose Revolution?

There wasn't a lot of doctrinaire mumbo-jumbo in our music, and I think that was resented.
Rob Tyner, interviewed by Ben Edmonds, 1990

It's 1968. Politicos and peaceniks march against America's meddling in Vietnam. Anti-war factions in the US and Europe spring up and down like whack-a-mole. Modus operandi vary: megaphone diplomacy; cop-baiting street scuffles; improvised, I'm-mad-me eccentricity. For many, only dialogue will stem the flow of body bags. Some throw stones, or worse. A few devolve to clownish mischief, from exorcising the bad juju in the Defense Department to nominating a pig named Pigasus for President.

Whether the best way to bring the boys home was to petition the politicians, tear down the walls or levitate the Pentagon was moot. For MC5, it was academic: the revolution was abstract, conceptual, a vessel for rock 'n' roll, not vice-versa. The 5 had flirted with the usual touchstones of 1950s-60s protest: *Das Kapital*, Che Guevara posters, Ho Chi Minh cufflinks, whatever. But while the era's more strident protestors and academicians took MC5 to their hearts as shock-troops of the resistance, the band's onstage musical blitzkreig flattered to deceive. MC5 were no more far-left political attack-dogs than Ted Nugent was a pacifist. Despite hand-me-down wisdom inherited from John Sinclair and a coterie of ideological exhibitionists, anyone back in 1968 looking to MC5 as a radical lodestar would have been disappointed. Tying the 5 to the coming crisis of Western capitalism was like calling Frank Zappa a hippie; violent upheaval wasn't on their bucket list, even if they played what many took to be its soundtrack.

The 5's aggression in concert suggested another hotline to their closest musical inspirations. Pete Townshend may have hoped to die before he got old enough to write a rock opera, but while The Who's creative lead fed his fury into some of the stormiest rock music ever heard, the composer of 'My Generation' and 'Substitute' was no placard-waving politico. More auto-destructive art project than Oxford Union debate or Grosvenor Square riot, Townshend's anger felt existential and arbitrary, its target anything the establishment threw at him. Like Marlon Brando's in *The Wild One*, Pete's negativism proposed no solution, and he held in contempt evangelising, self-styled radicals and holier-than-thou activists. Witness his peremptory dispatch of Abbie Hoffman when the Youth International Party leader tried to muscle in on The Who's show at Woodstock, of which more later.

In their earliest years, MC5 were kicking down the fence because it was there, not because the neighbours had all the local gossip on a better world. And in truth, little would change before the band called time in 1972. Having toed John Sinclair's party line and assumed the position with dutiful seditionary aplomb, the 5 later insisted they never bought their manager's faux-militancy and magical thinking, still less the gurning tomfoolery of histrionic provocateurs like Hoffman and fellow late-1960s nuisances Jerry Rubin and Paul Krassner. As for the routine misreading of MC5's famous signature tune, America's middle classes were better advised to lock up their daughters than unlock the gun cupboard. The only armed struggle MC5 had on their minds was feverish, sweaty, adolescent sex. 'I only wanted to be in a rock and roll band,' Mike Davis mused. 'This crusade to forge a new world seemed ludicrous, a Quixotic lunge at an imaginary adversary.' In 1990, Rob Tyner reminded Ben Edmonds, of *Creem* and *Rolling Stone*, how rarely, to Sinclair's chagrin, insurrectionary rhetoric was admitted into their songwriting. As later recorded in the essential *MC5: An Oral Biography of Rock's Most Revolutionary Band* (2024) by Edmonds, Brad Tolinski and Jaan Uhelszki, Rob lamented how the 5 had become 'artists under a quasi-Maoist regime':

> In Mao's China, art was to be subjugated [to] political message and propaganda, and we weren't always playing that game.

The MC5 story began in Lincoln Park: part of the archipelago of working-class communities in Metro Detroit which the city's parvenus dismissed as 'Downriver'. As Wayne Kramer wrote: 'The Summer of Love didn't make a stop in Detroit. It didn't fit.' Just as the post-industrial good earth of the English Midlands would propagate such bad apples as The Move, Black Sabbath, Mott The Hoople, Slade, Judas Priest, Napalm Death, half of Led Zeppelin and three-quarters of The Pretenders, MC5 were welded to the Motor City like fairings on a Ford Fairlane. Peace and love never stood an earthly among the shop floors, chicken stands and downtown dive bars of Detroit, so where better than the birthplace of the pumped-up muscle car to bear the ultimate in virile, high-octane US rock 'n' roll? Where else but America's once-thriving industrial heart, soon to be listed for life support, could more decisively convince young, frustrated musicians to take up arms?

Between 1910 and 1940, Detroit was among the northern industrial hubs to attract the first Great Migration from the Deep South of people soon to identify as African-American. Only a relative lack of professional recording facilities prevented the immediate arrival of electric urban blues to rival its fertile Midwestern neighbour, Chicago. Then by the late 1940s, Detroit's massively expanding auto industry, with its opportunities for jobs and growth, was fuel-injecting America's post-war prosperity. The black diaspora was now an ineluctable part of the Motor City community. A thriving music recording industry could only follow.

During a fortnight of dates in December 1947 backing Sarah Vaughan at Detroit's El Sino Club, Charlie Parker was asked to cut a few sides by Savoy Records. Keen to avoid a time-consuming drive back to the Windy City, where he'd be obliged to weather a pay-related union ban on commercial recording activities, the bebop giant's quintet checked in at United Sound Systems on Second Avenue. The state-of-the-art setup impressed Parker's group, and word spread. Detroit-out-of-Clarksdale bluesman John Lee Hooker arrived to cut his seminal 'Boogie Chillen', and United's reputation was sealed as a centre of excellence for the recording industry. And Detroit's own, as a hotbed of fierce musical creativity, was ignited.

Towards the end of the 1950s, over at 2648 West Grand Boulevard, an enterprising songwriter, record producer and former boxer, Berry Gordy Jr, was busy signing talented young black singers and instrumentalists to a new imprint. Gordy had spotted the commercial advantage to be had in sweetening the hard-edged blues percolating up from the Delta with the comfort food of R&B, doo-wop and gospel. Alongside Smokey Robinson, Jackie Wilson and Al Green (no relation to the famously reverential singer), he raised a thrilling new strain of slick, dancefloor-filling black pop-soul, which an international audience lapped up and eventually put millions of bucks into the Tamla Motown label chief's pocket. That Berry was as shrewd a capitalist entrepreneur as any car-plant CEO was no hindrance. As Hitsville USA thrived, he had the smarts to tack the production-line ethos of the auto industry onto a sleek recording business model with no loss of forward momentum, fuel efficiency or sexy, chromium-plated pizzazz.

Yet Gordy's achievements (some would say off the backs of his artists, but never within earshot of his lawyers) proved a paradox. For here was a prosperous black businessman, his fortune founded on tailoring indigenous music to the widest possible market, operating in a town where the rise of automated process – just one aspect of the forces of capitalism – was eroding prospects for thousands of black workers. Only a select few were lucky and talented enough to escape food stamps and the assembly line and become household names with Tamla Motown. Yet motorvating through Metro Detroit like a demolition derby, holding a darkly combative mirror to Motown's relatively unthreatening image, were a tough bunch of white rockers. The Stooges, Ted Nugent's Amboy Dukes, Bob Seger, The Up, Suzi Quatro's pre-Chinnichap band The Pleasure Seekers, The Scott Richard Case, Mitch Ryder & The Detroit Wheels, Grand Funk Railroad, Alice Cooper and – above all – MC5 stepped up and spoke to a harsher, swarf-under-the-fingernails realism. It was all nailgunned into a growing antiwar, anti-establishment pugnacity, giving Motor City rock 'n' roll a sense of identity to rival that of New York, Los Angeles or San Francisco.

It's 1963. Wayne Kramer (b Wayne Stanley Kambes, Detroit, 30 April 1948) lures high-school buddy Fred Smith (b Frederick Dewey Smith, Lincoln County W. Virginia, 14 September 1948) away from The Vibratones to play bongos with his new band. The Bounty Hunters are a Ventures-style surf outfit christened by Wayne, like so many Motor City dudes a racing fan, after the nickname of dragstrip legend Connie Kalitta. At the bidding of his future lead vocalist, Wayne will change his own surname to something easier on the tongue: 'Kramer' sounds good: a consumer product, a brand of cheese, or a vacuum cleaner. This appeals to the all-American boy lurking within this radical novitiate. He'll also distance himself from his long-absent father and an unhappy, abusive adolescence at the wandering hands of his stepfather. Fred's working-class background is similarly difficult. He's lived in Detroit since he was young, his dad securing factory work after moving the Smiths up from the south. As both teenagers discover the healing power of music, Fred switches to bass and lines up with Wayne, second guitarist Billy Vargo and drummer Leo LeDuc. Thus assembled, the prototype MC5 is rolling out of the factory gates.

Growing interest in and around town encouraged the boys to leave their jobs and seek work as a professional group. Like many young axemen, Wayne was weaned on guitar-based instrumentals by Duane Eddy, Link Wray, The Ventures and Johnny & The Hurricanes. He spent hours diligently pulling apart and reconstructing Rolling Stones songs and Chuck Berry solos. But as he told *Rolling Stone* in 2014, as appealing as the usual suspects was the edgy, paradigm-busting jazz known as New Thing:

Pharoah Sanders, Archie Shepp, John Coltrane and Sun Ra – that's what originally inspired me and MC5. What the most advanced jazz musicians were doing was pushing the music forward, and that was my goal as a rock player in MC5. I needed a source of inspiration that was unorthodox and provocative on every level. I had reached a point where I could play the guitar okay ... Sun Ra showed me where to go from there.

New Thing is usually held to have begun in 1959, when Ornette Coleman (de)tuned his plastic alto sax, mobilised a freewheeling quartet and occupied New York City's Five Spot club, there to blow away the remaining shards from the mainstream music Charlie Parker had begun shattering fifteen years earlier. After Coleman formalised free jazz in 1960 with a famously eponymous album, this furious audial reaction to mounting American racism became the default *cri de coeur* for numerous angry young musicians. Coleman, Albert Ayler, Archie Shepp and Pharoah Sanders lined up with the slightly older Eric Dolphy, John Coltrane, Cecil Taylor and Sun Ra to face down the bigotry grimly metastasising across the US, their wrath vented in long, roiling sheets of liquid fire. Occasionally incoherent but often exhilarating, this sonic decomposition was the vengefully authentic voice of downtrodden, disenfranchised black America, as volatile as Public Enemy and NWA decades later. As Shepp intimated to *Down Beat* magazine in 1964, his tenor saxophone was the nearest he could get to a Vietcong fighter's machine gun.

As they strapped on their guitars, Wayne Kramer and Fred Smith summoned a similar spirit. Each shared a love of the musically adventurous, alongside conventional blues, R&B and classically adolescent rock 'n' roll. A racetrack pal of Wayne's, Robert W. Derminer (b Detroit, 12 December 1944), despite high-school graduation photos predicting middle-American contentment as a plump, bespectacled Pontiac accounts clerk, was known among local scenesters as a hip political thinker, an intellectual beatnik straight from the pages of Kerouac or Burroughs. At a burger bar early one morning in 1964, Wayne encountered Robert (then widely assumed an unwaveringly purist jazz fan) drunkenly wailing away on a harmonica and raving about The Rolling Stones. The guitarist invited the apparent convert to manage The Bounty Hunters. Vargo and LeDuc quit, Fred took over on rhythm guitar and Bob Gaspar joined as drummer. Wayne asked his new manager to play bass alongside the clerical duties, but Derminer was blessed with a fine soulboy voice and, despite an incipient tubbiness and a gap-toothed but winningly cheeky smile, had charisma aplenty. Once Rob had proved he could own a stage as commandingly – if not quite as fluently – as an Otis Redding or a James Brown, he took to front-of-house, and Patrick Burrows joined on bass.

Derminer renamed himself in homage to John Coltrane's pianist, McCoy Tyner, adding the 'Sonic' to Fred Smith and, later, the 'Machine Gun' to Dennis Thompson. Now Robin Tyner, the singer also honoured Detroit ancestry by suggesting the group be rechristened The Motor City 5. In turn, this was contracted to MC5, recalling an auto-part product code, the British Invasion group The Dave Clark Five (DC5) and, insisted Rob, Einstein's Special Theory of Relativity: the scientific absolute the new band would spend the next few years doing their best to shatter.

Still teenagers, MC5 rehearsed in Wayne's mother's basement. They retooled Stones and Yardbirds songs to take on the road to parties, barbeques and high-school sock hops. They toured teen shacks such as the Hideout, Daniel's Den and the Y-A-Go-Go. As Rob confessed to Ben Edmonds: 'Playing gigs wasn't about money. It was mostly about picking up chicks.' A local acquaintance, Bruce Bennington, offered to help as a roadie-factotum, driving the group to gigs and enjoying the prestige of hanging out with cool rock 'n' rollers. But with the 5 desperate for new equipment, the unworldly Bruce ill-advisedly fronted Wayne a bank loan, funding two 100-watt Vox Super Beatle tube guitar amplifiers, chrome stands, a sixty-watt bass amp and a T60 bass cabinet. The rig enabled MC5, then rubbing along on no jobs, no money and Wayne's fifteen-watt Epiphone amp, to boost the volume and clarity of their live music to many times those of their peer groups. While Kramer later conceded that MC5 had taken unfair advantage of Bennington, the lure of high living and groupie action went only so far; their patron's naïveté would dry up after the 5 failed to make the monthly loan repayments.

Even as Wayne rehearsed his chops, he was hustling local promoters for gigs. He discovered that most managers and bookers at Detroit's myriad small live-music clubs preferred bland covers bands to street gangs with guitars crashing out original, if indigestible material. Inspired by the new sounds fashioned by English guitarists such as Townshend and Jeff Beck, the 5's leader experimented with volume, distortion and feedback while Rob began writing lyrics. In his autobiography, *The Hard Stuff*, Kramer described an epiphany:

[Townshend and Beck] were doing the most advanced things with the electric guitar, and I was way into it. I set my guitar down at rehearsal with the volume up and left the room. I heard this unholy howling sound coming from the basement, and then a crash. A jar of nails sitting on a shelf had vibrated off and broken on the floor. I told the guys, 'I've discovered the power to change the universe: feedback'.

Unmoved, Burrows and Gaspar deferred to the club owners, alienated by what John Sinclair would label MC5's 'avant-rock'. After somewhat prefabricated censure from Wayne and Fred for replacing his Höfner violin bass with a Fender Precision, Pat stormed out of a rehearsal with a terse 'fuck you'. Enter Michael Davis (b Detroit, 5 June 1943), whom Rob had met when the singer's girlfriend and later wife, Becky, lived near Mike in a Wayne State Uni campus flophouse called the Balmoral Hotel. (On joining the 5, Mike bought a new bass guitar, declining a Höfner in favour of a Fender Precision; ironically, Wayne and Fred approved.) Gaspar, meanwhile, had to choose between a life of rock 'n' roll debauchery as MC5's drummer and his day job at a local bank. One night in mid-gig, as Davis recorded in his autobiography, *I Brought Down MC5*, Fred launched into a guitar drone the 5 had been tossing around in rehearsals, and which Gaspar was known to loathe:

To Bob, it was not a song, not music, nothing but noise. Fred played and played, though, and Bob sat at his drums with stubborn resolve, refusing to accompany him. Soon the rest of us joined Fred, droning away in this never-ending pulse, Rob shaking his maracas and stepping around at the front like a tribal shaman. Rob began to sing, 'Let your love come down, baby, in the midnight hour ...' All at once, with the angriest look he could muster, Bob cranked off a long single stroke roll into the song that sent shock waves through the room, and we were off!

Bob, too, was off, back to the financial sector. The racket that so spooked the drummer prototyped a song that would establish MC5's direction of travel and become a lengthy, savagely anthemic show-closer. Its title, 'Black To Comm', suggested a political red light, something to do with black people and communists, presumably. As with 'kick out the jams', the truth was more prosaic. Tyner explained to Ben Edmonds the reasoning behind the open-ended onslaught MC5 would later nickname 'The Hydrogen Bomb':

It was always a chore to set up the PA in those days. You had to connect all the little wires, and connecting the black wire to the ground, which was 'comm', was essential. So 'Black To Comm' was the connection that allowed our whole sound to happen.

Rob added that the band's musical style was a consequence of its fiery genesis in a discordant industrial landscape on borrowed time:

You're always screaming in this fucking town. We grew up in this city that was being built up and torn down at the same time. There was all this turbulence and turmoil everywhere you went, and the cars were loud and real fast. We tried to express all of that in our music, especially in songs like 'Black To Comm'.

To replace Gaspar, MC5 invited Dennis Thompson (b Dennis Andrew Tomich, Lincoln Park, Detroit, 7 September 1948), a boyhood friend of Wayne's and one-time Bounty Hunter. Bitingly outspoken, Thompson had depped with the 5 and possessed his own set of Ludwigs, which he would attack with the power, speed, aggression and abandon that suited MC5's unwritten ethos. 'My first impressions of Dennis were exactly as predicted,' wrote Davis. 'He was cranky and high strung, always in a foul mood, and he bitched about anything that rubbed him the wrong way.'

At last, the full-bore, high-test MC5.

Kramer remembered the Stones coming to Detroit in 1965: 'We were supposed to open for them,' Wayne told Edmonds, 'but got knocked out of the box at the last minute. That was a real heartbreaker.' As he wrote in *The Hard Stuff*: 'We were aced out of the gig by another local band that featured an eleven year old drummer. Plus, the kid's father knew the promoter, and that was that.'

Losing the gig may also have been due to the 5's habit, common among many, of seasoning their early live set with too many Stones covers. Now MC5 were coerced into creating original material. New songs would become stage classics, sometimes involving the lively saxophone coloratura appropriated from New Thing, played by Wayne, or Sonic, or eventually the Coltrane-fixated Sinclair. Among these songs was 'Black To Comm', which would not appear on record until long after the band had split.

Rob's promotion from manager to vocalist created a vacancy. At a Detroit radio station, WKNR, the 5 were introduced to 'Swinging' Sweeney, a local deejay keen to get into pop management. Wayne thought he was a jerk, but everyone liked Swinging's vivacious, multitalented partner. Apparently Boudicca crossbred with Annie Oakley, British expat Ann Marston was a singer, a horsewoman, a Miss Michigan and, from 1949 to 1960, a US archery champion. Seeing The Beatles in 1964 inspired Ann to promote shows and, eventually, to get one over on her boyfriend by managing several groups in the Detroit area, among them The Lower Deck, The Satellites and MC5. Before ill-health forced her to quit – Ann once broke three ribs in a rodeo and later contracted Type-1 diabetes, which would take her sight – she booked the band to open for The Dave Clark Five at Cobo Hall in front of an audience of fifteen thousand, the biggest date of the 5's career so far. 'We hated Sweeney, but we loved Ann,' Wayne wrote in his memoir. 'She was a beautiful grown woman and we all wanted to sleep with her.' Whether any or all of the band succeeded remains gallantly unspoken.

MC5 continued to court media contacts. Ann's management duties were now assumed by three 'small-time music business hustlers': an MGM promos man, Cliff Gordon; a Detroit 'character' called Larry Benjamin; and Arnold Mark Geller, an exec whose initials gave the trio's tiny record company its name. AMG booked MC5 into Tera Shirma, a Detroit studio where Motown's chief engineer, Russ Terrana, apprenticed following guitar duties with the pre-Rare Earth covers outfit The Sunliners. First to tape was 'Gloria', a three-chord garage shriek penned by an eighteen year old Van Morrison for Them, an angry bunch of Brit-invasion Belfast toughs. As a nicely annealed staple of MC5's live set, 'Gloria' was a shoo-in maiden single. But as Thompson lamented in 2006 to 5 biographer Brett Callwood:

A band out of Chicago called The Shadows of Knight beat us to it. The very same week we were going into the studio to record ['Gloria'], it came on the radio. We were pretty shook up over that … They beat us by a couple of months, which is a bitch.

MC5 instead chose another live favourite repurposed from Them, 'I Can Only Give You Everything', written by Phil Coulter and Tommy Scott. The 5 cut the single in late 1966 for release in the New Year. With The Shadows of Knight's 'Gloria' proving gossamer-thin compared with Them's weightily clamorous original, the 5 were determined to prove a point. Their new reading of 'I Can Only Give You Everything' was hard as nails, the sound of the Motor City sexed up on Red Ginseng and Spanish Fly. With little producers' input other than from Tera Shirma's capable but indifferent technicians – an engineer scolded Kramer for excessive distortion before the guitarist insisted that was the whole point – MC5's debut was driven by a massive fuzztone guitar riff and dramatic reverb, as if Morrison's group, themselves no slouches when it came to rama-lama R&B, had been zapped with a shot of undiluted battery acid and hooked up to a Chrysler 426. On the flip, 'One Of The Guys' was MC5's first original to make it to vinyl: a robust, Beatley casserole of distorted guitars, subterranean bass and Machine Gun's appropriately rat-a-tat snare fills. Its mood was rootsier still, as if the 5 had beamed down to the Cavern Club c1962 to support The Big Three. Tyner's lyrics even evoked the Fabs and the Stones, as the singer told Ben Edmonds:

Before we moved to Detroit, we hung out at a White Castle in Lincoln Park [a burger franchise, possibly the branch where Wayne made Rob his fateful offer of employment], which was like the centre of our universe. The crowd liked The Beatles and the Stones, but they were still suspicious of people with long hair. I was growing my hair out and changing, so in some ways the lyrics were my attempt to say goodbye to that world: 'I don't see how you survive being one of the guys'.

Rob's metamorphosis and the new 45 were undoubtedly promising, but an indifferent nation snoozed. Meanwhile Gordon, Benjamin and Geller saw no irony in banning politics and drugs then expecting their clients to procure them weed. Nor did they flinch from trumpeting their formidable business acumen just as an eviction notice was served for defaulting on the office rent. 'They were nice enough guys,' Kramer wrote, 'but clearly there was no future for us with them.' A new manager's time was about to come.

John Sinclair (b Flint, Mitchigan, 3 October 1941) was a poet, journalist, BA in American Literature from the University of Michigan and a born political gadfly. Dropping his studies for an MA at Wayne State University, John co-founded the Detroit Artists' Workshop, the Wayne State University Artists' Society, the Artists' Workshop Press and, of particular resonance as MC5 fruited, a commune called Trans-Love Energies Unlimited. A tireless networker with impeccable connections, as addicted to music, marijuana and mayhem as he was to prose, poetry and politics, Sinclair could procure top quality reefer from his jazz contacts at a time when personal use of even small quantities, let alone dealing, could have life-changing legal consequences. His marketing strategies would be his undoing: in October 1964, he fell for a sting by an undercover narcotics agent and was fined $400 for possession, with two years' probation. Eighteen months later, after pleading guilty to possession and avoiding a heavier penalty for selling, Sinclair was sent away to the DHC for six months. More would be coming – and it would seriously affect the development of MC5.

John emerged from prison that August to an all-day welcome-home party. The 'Festival of People' was thrown by John's wife, Leni, at the Artists' Workshop. Founded in November 1964 and spread over seven cheap, inner-city rental houses near the Wayne State campus, the DAW was fulcrum of the Sinclairs' proto-insurrectionist activities and a crucible for youthful creative dissent: a place where the city's freaks, musicians, artists, filmmakers, painters, poets and potheads could further the revolution by reading Kropotkin and taking loads of drugs. As MC5 sought closer ties with Sinclair and the Workshop – they mainly needed a regular rehearsal space – the band showed up at the homecoming, hoping to curry favour with the power couple. Not unreasonably, the returnee had more pressing matters as the missus tarried upstairs. 'We had waited all day to play for him,' Kramer recounted in 1997 to Fred Goodman, author of *The Mansion On The Hill*, 'then at two in the morning they finish with all the fucking poetry ... and we cranked the shit up.'

Unfortunately the shit was only cranked up for three songs before Leni, by now as aroused as much by MC5 as by her husband and – coincidentally – a neighbour at the door with a shotgun, rushed downstairs to shut off the power. John was incensed by the ruckus these tykes had been making in his house, and was soon excoriating rock 'n' roll and all its works in 'The Coat Puller', his regular column on the Detroit underground paper *The Fifth Estate*. Rob Tyner, by now a firm convert to rock music and how it might merge with free jazz, responded with an opinion piece of his own. The pair bonded over booze, weed and Cecil Taylor, and Sinclair resolved to experience the band without distraction. He described to Ben Edmonds his feelings about first seeing MC5 (at a battle of the bands in Northville) while noting the landmines the 5 apparently couldn't resist sewing along the path ahead:

> When they did 'Black To Comm', man, that fucking killed me. When I met them, they didn't really have a show. They were raggedy and nothing was together. They had some guy doing their equipment who just fumbled around. They'd be late, their gig would be a mess, then they'd play a handful of tunes and go into a half-hour version of 'Black To Comm', and this would be in a teen club. Everybody hated it, but not me.

Sinclair agreed informally to advise the band and allow them space at DAW to rehearse. For the 5's live show, Kramer had taken his lead both from Shepp, Sanders *et al* and from James Brown; in 1965, when Wayne attended seven successive nights' screenings of Brown's documentary film *The T.A.M.I. Show*, the theatricality of the Godfather of Funk's performance had transfixed the guitarist. Kramer told Goodman:

> Our show was based on the dynamic of James's show. It was going to start at ten-and-a-half and go up from there. On a bad night, we were going to be great – and on a good night, we were going to be unbelievable.

It's autumn 1966. Russ Gibb, a Dearborn middle-school teacher and part-time deejay, is introduced to the 5 at the Artists' Workshop by local jazz drummer and deejay Jerry Goodwin. On his radio programme in 1969, Russ will peddle rock's most fatuous conspiracy fantasy, the 'death' of Paul McCartney. For now, the ambitious entrepreneur seeks a house band for the new Detroit rock venue he's decided to launch after seeing The Byrds at San Francisco's Fillmore Auditorium. Within three months, he's taken a lease on the Grande Ballroom, a Moorish Art Deco theatre at 8952 Grand River Avenue; hired Gary Grimshaw, a friend of Rob Tyner, to design publicity posters; tasked artist and head-shop manager Robin Sommers with running strobes and a liquified light show; and booked MC5 to play every Friday and Saturday night. For this, he'll pay the princely fee of $125.

Sinclair relocated DAW from an old dental surgery with a street-side shopfront to another rental property a few blocks away. He rebranded the Workshop Trans-Love Energies Unlimited, after a lyric from Donovan's song 'The Fat Angel'. John and Leni had recently returned from a mind-altering sabbatical in Switzerland, where they visited the Sandoz Laboratory, birthplace of LSD, a popular commodity among habitués of the rewired DAW. Trans-Love Energies would, in effect, be an urban precursor of that tent at Woodstock where festivalgoers recovered from the brown acid; an alternative colony, purveyor of soulfood and free healthcare clinics, organiser of weekly free outdoor concerts, publisher of underground newssheets and a haven in which to smoke, crash and avoid the law. The motto at Trans-Love was Serve The People, or STP; as the Woodstock yurt's wasted would note a couple of years later, the initials also represented a turbocharged hallucinogen then popular in San Francisco.

TLE's first organised gathering was Detroit's answer to San Fran's famously loved-up Human Be-In of January 1967. It proved among the more unlovely of bad trips, attaching permanent targets to the backs of both MC5 and the Trans-Love enterprise. Held at Belle Isle on the Detroit River on 30 April 1967 – Wayne's birthday – the event was an outdoor concert featuring MC5, The Up, Seventh Seal and Billy C. & The Sunshine. At around 7pm, the 5 weighed into 'Black To Comm'. A well-refreshed member of Outlaws MC was arrested, angry bikers started harassing the audience and the good vibes quickly soured. 150 mounted police officers needed no further excuse, indiscriminately laying into the crowd with billyclubs and tear gas as thousands fled the island. Although only around a dozen were arrested, MC5 and Trans-Love were now tagged as dangerous troublemakers. Much worse was to come.

Early on Sunday, 23 July on Detroit's Near West Side, police raided a 'blind pig', an after-hours shebeen with a mainly black clientele. Three youths were slain in the melee by white cops. The resulting unrest escalated into eight straight days of some of the USA's bloodiest urban violence, involving police, the National Guard and the 82nd and 101st Airborne divisions. In what became known as the 12th Street Riots (or the colloquially anodyne and romanticised 'Detroit Uprising') 43 people were killed, 1,189 injured, more than 7,000 were arrested and some 400 buildings were levelled. During a lengthy period of nationwide racial discord – Newark had exploded a week earlier, and the fury would sweep across state lines long into 1968 – America had suffered nothing on such a scale since the Civil War.

Perversely, John Sinclair professed himself delighted. 'Oh man, it's exhilarating,' he gushed to Brett Callwood, with casual, off-the-pigs predictability. 'We wanted a confrontation with the authorities and we wanted them to lose.' Wayne Kramer was more circumspect, questioning the motives rather than basking in urban calamity: 'The people of Detroit who had been on the short end of the stick for so long,' he wrote in his 2018 memoir, 'lashed out at everything that represented the generations of racism and poverty they had endured.' Dennis Thompson was unimpressed by Sinclair's royal 'we': 'It was scary, very much so. Bullets were flying and tanks were driving down the street. It was dangerous, people died.'

MC5 were hardly waterproofed from the riots' backwash, despite Trans-Love's cossetting. Helped along by an aggressively badgering police department, the band's equipment truck was trashed. If the dibbles ventured anywhere near the Grande, the 5's earsplitting stage show conveniently invited charges of disturbing the peace. When finally TLE's premises at Warren and John C. Lodge were firebombed, followed in April 1968 by Martin Luther King's assassination in Memphis, MC5, their WAGs and Sinclair's entire nomenklatura decamped to Ann Arbor, a relatively tranquil oblast one hour from Detroit. Now based at Hill House, a rented mansion at 1510 Hill Street, the Trans-Love operation could refocus its fevered energies on music and the blessed struggle.

Sinclair also finally agreed to look after MC5 as de facto manager (although the status was obviously bourgeois, and no contracts were signed; on the 5's forthcoming first album, he'd be credited vaguely with 'guidance'). He told Jason Gross about how, in August 1967, he'd been inspired by The Grateful Dead, then dating at the Grande. According to many in sooty Michigan the Dead were typical Californian lotus eaters, but John was moved by the band's managers:

I hung out with Rock Scully and Danny Rifkin for a few days. I thought, man, these guys are just as nuts as I am. They have a band that's on Warner Brothers and they're on a national tour. It must be possible to do this.

Despite his instinctive jazzer's suspicions of rock 'n' roll, Sinclair reasoned MC5 had the potential to become one of the biggest bands – and, by association, revolutionary influencers – in the US. So he began shaping his unofficial clients according to what he foresaw the homeland becoming. At first his ambitions for the 5 looked promising. Despite the right-on affectations, he had a real nose for business. He did a standup job of insulating the band from the more po-faced, but important, commercial elements of rock 'n' roll the 5 had so little time for. He supervised transportation, sourced an ancient Chevy van and decorated it with MC5 livery, treated with promoters, recruited helpers, hustlers and fellow travellers, oversaw booking arrangements and ensured the band were onstage within reasonable time of a venue shutting for the night. He also looked after equipment and amplification, which was useful: immediately after a June 1967 gig supporting Jefferson Airplane at Ford Auditorium, erstwhile 5 benefactor and whipping boy Bruce Bennington stopped by with two Detroit cops and a court order, demanding repossession of all of the band's equipment apart from Dennis's drums.

On 4 January 1968, MC5 cut their second single. Produced by Sinclair, with Russ Gibb fronting the $500 studio bill, 'Looking At You' was released in March on A-Square, a small label run by charismatic Ann Arbor deejay and scenester Hugh 'Jeep' Holland. Written by Smith, Tyner and Davis, this two-chord, white-hot wonder would later be cleaned and pressed for MC5's second album. In its earlier state, however, 'Looking At You' had all the consumer-friendly smoothness of lysergic sandpaper, its guitars sounding like Wayne and Fred had tried to drive a fifteen-foot bus under a thirteen-foot bridge with Rob's vocal trapped on the smokers' deck. With the whole thing drizzled in enough feedback and distortion to rattle cavity fillings a mile away, MC5's sophomore 45 was astounding, a statement of intent that would become one of the band's most enduringly popular songs. 'Borderline', penned by Wayne and Mike, was as overdriven as its A-side, with the unusual distinction of sounding even scuzzier than its later live equivalent (taped in concert at the Grande, the piece would appear on the 5's first LP). Once again, Tyner attacked his mic as if providing Radio Shack repairers with a reason to live.

In May the 5 played at the Grosse Point Hideout. When Dennis Thompson and John Sinclair skived off outside the club to share a spliff, a bouncer dutifully shopped the pair to local police. The rest of the band were alerted, while roadie Ron Levine encouraged the audience to confront the cops. The club owner, seeking the early night and quiet life not usually specified on an MC5 booking, withdrew the charge. The 5's small victory intensified later that evening when the owner pulled the plug in an attempt to get everyone to leave. Fred led the crowd in a boisterous chant of 'Power! Power! Power!' until the electricity was returned, the band could complete their set and the owner could get to his bed. A week later at the Grande, MC5 were opening for Cream when Russ Gibb theatened to have the 5 arrested over a plan to burn the US flag onstage. Tyner instead raised a large banner emblazoned with a marijuana leaf. To a gale of feedback, a buck-naked lighting rigger marched to the front of the stage, sat down cross-legged and chanted 'Om'.

That August, the Democratic National Convention was convened in Chicago to anoint the next president. The event notoriously combined violent unrest with political buffoonery, as protestors strove to convince delegates that the USA's military-industrial complex wasn't such a good idea after all. Orchestrating the restlessness was energetic rent-a-riot Abbie Hoffman, who'd booked some of America's most vocal anti-war stars to perform at his free Festival of Life, scheduled for the day before the convention. Abbie's plans went awry after he failed to obtain permits for Arlo Guthrie, Country Joe & The Fish, Phil Ochs and The Fugs. Others rumoured to have signed, only to bail just before the show, were the Dead, Airplane, Dylan, the Stones and even, it was said, The Beatles. Since MC5 somehow fell through the licensing officials' net, the most dangerously abrasive band of the lot were able to take a clear run at the 3,000 kids waiting expectantly in Chicago's Lincoln Park.

Sinclair later recorded how he asked co-organiser Ed Sanders for electricity to the 5's amps, which were set up on the back of a flatbed truck, Grateful Dead-style. The Fugs' poet-in-residence pleaded a feed from a nearby concessionaire, although how the Dead's famously huge backline might have coped with the power surge from a hotdog stand has never been calculated. MC5, by now all baked off their tits on hash cookies, played for just under an hour. They finished upon the arrival of Mayor Richard Daley's riot cops, who'd enjoyed busting heads all week and were surely drooling at the prospect of Hoffman's (unrealised) plot to spike the city's water supply with acid. Undeterred, the Yippie leader grabbed a mic and started wanging on about 'pigs' and 'the seige of Chicago'. MC5 were packed up and headed back to Detroit by the time the tear gas rolled in.

At first Sinclair was dismayed to see his plans for national exposure and political kudos for MC5 sunk, not least by the am-dram absurdities of his own people – in this case, the communards from Festival of Life. John later told Ben Edmonds of the futility of hooking up with individuals who would eventually be dismissed as 'Groucho Marxists': 'I realised [Hoffman and co] had no grasp of street-level reality at all.' Yet Sinclair's own card was marked by no less a treasured national pest than Country Joe McDonald, who quietly took Tyner aside to counsel against exploitative chancers. As Rob told Edmonds:

> He was talking about John Sinclair and the rest of the politicos. He said, 'Man, me and my band used to go to all these goddamn benefits and look what it got me. We got out there and we got used and abused. And that's what's happening to you ... These people will bleed you till you can't stand up and won't ever say thank you; they'll just throw you away like tissue paper.'

Sinclair was busy fretting over the band's image. Shortly after the DNC, Pulitzer prize-winner Norman Mailer, a veteran of 1967's 'levitate the Pentagon' protest, smithed a piece on MC5 for *Harper's* magazine which, a few months later, only *Rolling Stone*'s young Eric Ehrmann would outdo for colloquial overkill. 'Had the horns of the Hun ever had noise to compare?' Mailer pantingly enquired, before likening MC5's Hunlike noise to 'an electric crescendo screaming as if at the electro-mechanical climax of the age.' It may have been deafened as much by Norman's mixed metaphors as MC5's Mosrite-generated decibels, but a nation was waking from its slumber.

On 1 November 1968, Sinclair took up the white man's burden by announcing the birth of Trans-Love's political progeny, the White Panther Party. Keen to make nice with the Black Panther Party, a radical, Marxist-Leninist organisation founded in 1966, Sinclair bagman Lawrence 'Pun' Plamondon had met BP senior management during a 90-day sleepover in the jug. With the cautious approval of the new group's near-namesakes, the happy event was solemnised with a ten-point manifesto. High on the wish list were the aforementioned 'total assault on the culture', an end to money and free ... well, everything, from private ownership to prisoners, with the abolition of capitalism a useful bonus. Filtered through the dark energy of MC5, Sinclair's screed would be inscribed on tablets of stone, the revolution a mere rock's throw away.

Forming a cabinet seemed to be based on whoever was in the room at the time. The verbose Sinclair was Minister of Information; Pun, a firearms enthusiast and the first hippie to make the FBI's 'Top Ten Most Wanted' list, was elected Minister of Defence; Pun's wife Genie became Minister of International Affairs. Sinclair generously included MC5 in his inner sanctum: Tyner accepted the Culture portfolio, while the others made do by sharing a diced-up Ministry of War. It all sounded laughably self-important: 'They gave our road manager, Steve 'The Hawk' Harnadek, the title of Minister of Fucking in the Streets,' Tyner remarked to Edmonds. 'Try and say that with a straight face.'

Yet finding common cause with America's foremost black-consciousness militants transcended the idle pretentions of needy honkies clinging to more credible revolutionary coattails. At least for now, the Black Panthers would tolerate like-minded emissaries from beyond the ghetto. Indeed, Sinclair's latest soviet was endorsed by none other than BP co-chairs Fred Hampton and Huey P. Newton. However, as heirs to an American ethnicity ceaselessly bludgeoned by Jim Crow laws and cops-Klan brutality, the Black Panthers already had real, painful skin in the game. Since it was nigh impossible to divorce the WPP from Abbie Hoffman's Yippies and similar cloddishness, the Brothers later dismissed their Caucasian would-be comrades as ineffectual 'psychedelic clowns'.

In 2018, Wayne peered through a half century's-worth of rose-tinted hindsight to try and explain the White Panthers. Couching a moderate argument in reason and common sense – a position that John Sinclair might have found hard to stomach – he assured Jim Kerr:

> [The White Panthers] gave us a voice to express our frustration with the slow pace of change. I felt that everything I did was patriotic at its core. Democracy requites participation – if you don't like the way something is, do whatever you need to do to get your ideas across. If it means putting pressure on elected leaders, put pressure on 'em. If it means voting the people you don't like out and those you do like in, there's something to do there. I felt that was what we were trying to do, correcting the ship of state.

Plotting the course of righteousness was clearly in Sinclair's mind when he revealed his next brainwave. An 'ecumenical psychedelic religion' according to Leni, the Church of Zenta added metaphysical elevation to the earnestness of the WPP, the ritual consumption of cannabis and other powders, preparations and paint thinners high on its catechism. With the political concept of separation of powers either too arcane or not worth the bother, the White Panthers at prayer convoked as their High Priest the WPP's ranking Minister of Religion and MC5 roadie, Jesse 'J. C.' Crawford. Leni revered the divine J. C. as a prophet sent from God, which must have been handy, given his spirituality was tested nightly by the weight of MC5's monolithic speaker cabinets. Now Zenta (or Zanta – as with any good ecumenical psychedelic religion, no one seemed sold on its precise spelling) sent forth their prophet to materialise before the supplicants at the beginning of every MC5 gig, a calling Brother Jesse pursued with the combined spiritual eagerness of a James Brown emcee, a fairground barker and a jiveass Pentecostal preacher.

Despite Kramer's later rationale, the entire DAW/TLE/White Panthers/Zenta pantomime, fountainhead of Rob Tyner's vividly expressed 'doctrinaire mumbo-jumbo', was looking less like rock 'n' roll by the day. Other TLE-affiliated bands, such as The Up, along with queues of camp-followers, toadies and grifters, came to regard MC5 as an unquestioning, deep-pocketed meal ticket, and sponged accordingly. As Dennis Thompson told Legs McNeil, this wasn't why he joined up: 'We were treated like good little communists, but I'd rather be a great drummer in a great rock 'n' roll band.' He reminded Brett Callwood: 'If I wanted to be a political person I would go back to college.'

While Sinclair prepped his cohort for a bravely collectivist future as sonic midwives to the revolution, the drift began: from the hormonal nonchalance of youngbloods who wanted nothing more than to get high, fuck and play rock 'n' roll louder, faster, heavier, dirtier and just damn better than anybody else; to the unquestioning, quasi-religious fervency of sermonising crusaders, fuelled by drugs that were now less recreational than sacramental.

Mike Davis sensed the proselytising was eroding the band's core values:

We were losing our identity as rock and roll hooligans. We smoked a lot of pot. We'd been smoking pot before, but this was different. John was taking on guru-like status, becoming our mentor and teacher. I felt uncomfortable in this atmosphere … It was as if we were about to become missionaries. We were no longer five individuals, making up an imprecise singular entity. We were now a community with a strategic socio-politico agenda, a strike force in the name of the underground.

Since this agitprop SWAT team still hadn't secured a record deal, Sinclair hyped MC5 around New York City. He was rebuffed until two *East Village Other* journalists and part-time deejays at New Jersey radio station WFMU, Dennis Frawley and Bob 'Righteous' Rudenick, introduced him to Danny Fields: fellow jock, future Ramones manager and, most importantly to MC5, publicity head/resident speedfreak with Elektra Records.

A folk-only label when it was started by Jac Holtzman in 1950, Elektra now recorded and marketed profitable rock groups (Paul Butterfield's Blues Band, Love, The Doors), reliably bankable troubadours (Judy Collins, Phil Ochs, Tim

Buckley) and left-field singularities (The Zodiac's *Cosmic Sounds*, Nico's glacial masterpiece *The Marble Index*). Impressed by Sinclair's pitch and already a likely consumer of Norman Mailer's hyperbole, Fields visited the Motor City to kick MC5's tyres. The band at the Grande was a life-changing experience for all concerned. Danny telephoned his boss with the glad tidings: MC5 were loud, wonderful, available and, most importantly, always polled profit-friendly audience numbers. Holtzman signed off an advance of $20,000, a further bargain-basement $5,000 securing, through the brokerage of Wayne Kramer, the 5's 'little brother band', The Psychedelic Stooges. After settling some debts and purchasing new equipment, MC5 and Sinclair marched downtown to a boutique called Louis the Hatter, there to confirm their solidarity with the overalls-wearing classes by buying expensive new leather coats.

Prodded by Sinclair and the 5, Elektra agreed to record the first album live at the Grande, a 'warm-up Wednesday' on 30 October 1968 to be followed by the real thing the night after. To encourage full houses, attendance at both gigs would be free, with The (soon no longer Psychedelic) Stooges opening. The timing was spiritually significant to Sinclair loyalists, if not MC5: the Church of Zenta decreed that 31 October would be its New Year. Besides the conventional mysticism of Halloween, the date marked Devil's Night, an annual Detroit festival of pranks and parties that usually deteriorated into city-wide arson and vandalism. The record company could care less. As far as Elektra was concerned, its exciting new signing was about to distil the town's gnarly essence into the toughest rock 'n' roll album of the year. And it would sell like Henry Ford's Model-fuckin'-Ts.

It's December 1968. Preview pressings of 'Kick Out The Jams', a new single culled from MC5's Devil's Night recordings, are doing the rounds. Confirming a full album release within two months, Elektra dispatches its clients to the East Coast for a short promo tour. MC5 spend three nights with The Velvet Underground at the Boston Tea Party, a popular Grande-style ballroom. Before the third show, Sinclair is tapped by a ragged 'anarchist arts collective' from New York called the Motherfuckers. Gatecrashing MC5's by now proprietorial use of the 'M' word, they're as uncompromising as their name, committed to violent social change or nothing. Abbie Hoffman wants to join, but he's thought not radical enough. Neither Sinclair nor MC5 know of the Motherfuckers' reputation. Nor could they guess that these cod-Trotskyite apparatchiks are about to denounce America's most inflammatory workingman's rock band as class traitors.

MC5 had won countercultural credit as the only musicians to play for the people outside the DNC. With the Motherfuckers' co-founder Ben Morea in police custody for stabbing a serviceman, his apostles walked among the 5 seeking after defence funds. Alrighty, agreed Sinclair, assuming the touchy commissars to be natural brothers-in-arms. John granted a Motherfucker permission to address the Tea Party audience in the interval. This presumption angered The Velvet Underground's irascible leader, Lou Reed, who demanded that MC5 fans leave forthwith on pain of his own band doing the same. Predictably, the appeal for money turned into a fuming philippic against the entire room. All music must be free, raged the spokes-Motherfucker, who chose not to dwell upon how the consequential loss of payment might affect his boss's legal bills. The Boston Tea Party was run by ripoff artists, he persisted, and now the bourgeoisie of Beantown must rise up and raze the entire place to the ground. Although the Motherfuckers were shooed away before anyone could short the glitterball, the venue's owner, Don Law, blamed MC5 for the intrusion and vowed that never again would the Detroiters darken his door. Law was not a man to cross; unbeknownst to the 5 or to Sinclair, the veteran music business executive and record producer subscribed to what effectively was a cartel of America's most influential music promoters: a boys' club that included the legendary – and legendarily ruthless – Bill Graham.

Over in NYC, Graham had his own issues with the Motherfuckers, who were cheerfully abusing a free weekly residency granted by the usually cautious impresario. More oddly still, given the events in Boston and the likely long-term consequences of Don Law's veto, Sinclair and MC5 agreed to play a free benefit gig for the Motherfuckers at Graham's storied venue, the Fillmore East, on 16 December. Apparently, this was a way to play nicely with 'the street people and our political comrades,' as Wayne, with rueful irony, later described the poseurs who would take a massive dump on his band next time their paths crossed.

Elektra pencilled another big MC5 Fillmore gig, supposedly Motherfucker-free, for 26 December. The Boston problems paled in comparison with an 'even bigger political shitstorm'. The Motherfuckers, who were shamelessly striping Graham for free tickets to the show, demanded that MC5 should refuse to play unless the promoter caved. Hostilities escalated, as Wayne wrote:

> Graham, a Holocaust survivor, was not a guy who submitted to extortion from neighbourhood thugs. Sinclair tried to mediate and got a number of tickets allocated for the locals, but this wasn't enough. The Motherfuckers were demonstrating out in front of the theatre when Graham confronted them. Someone hit Graham in the face with a chain, breaking his nose. Graham was certain it was Rob Tyner who assaulted him. I guess all white boys with Afros look alike. It wasn't Rob.

MC5 took to the boards before a packed house. At the mic, an innocent Tyner referenced the commotion outside: 'We didn't come to New York for politics, we came for rock 'n' roll.' This went down like a Molotov cocktail running on empty with the Motherfuckers, who promptly stormed the stage and began demolishing the 5's equipment. 'I watched as knives slashed through the fire curtain, while mayhem exploded out front,' Wayne wrote. 'Cymbals were crashing, amps were knocked over, and there was a lot of yelling and cursing.'

Danny Fields had planned to exfil MC5 from the combat zone in a hired stretch limousine. And aboard this resplendent symbol of everything the counterculture despised, waiting at the curb outside the theatre, retreated four of the 5. In 2002, Fields mitigated his apparent faux pas to *MOJO*:

> The band were seen as traitors to community values because I hired these limos. But I always did, because it made sense for large numbers of people. I was so naïve I didn't see it as a flagrantly provocative political gesture. I should have hired armored tanks.

None of this washed with the Motherfuckers. Deaf to Kramer's avowals that MC5 hadn't sold out to The Man, they went nuclear:

> I stood in the middle of East Sixth Street with the Motherfuckers ... screaming out all the Marxist polemical arguments at the top of their lungs. The neighbourhood nutcases, the speed freaks and junkies, bought into this and were adding the heavy vibes ... I saw the glint of a knife blade reflected in the streetlights. People were getting punched. I couldn't run, but it was becoming clear I couldn't stay either.

Like a secret-service detail protecting an imperilled president, two Motherfucker lieutenants bundled Wayne to relative safety and a cab back to the band's hotel. It was an abnormally thoughtful gesture that sealed one of MC5's more unfortunate episodes. Fallout from the debacle suggested that more holes than an empty ammo belt peppered the late-1960s militancy endorsed by quarrelsome agitprop groups, Sinclair and, with decreasing enthusiasm, MC5. Kramer later observed: '[The Motherfuckers] attacked their own comrades. We were on the same side, but they turned their revolutionary zeal against us.'

The Lower East Siders were not the only ones inconvenienced, however. The unhappiest outcome for MC5 that chaotic holiday season was two of America's most powerful music-industry figures, spuriously but damagingly, declaring the band persona non grata. Moreover, Laws and Graham advised their associates to blackball the 5 in solidarity. All MC5 needed for a full house were a pair of pissed record companies and a jailed manager, but those would come. Added to the backlashes following Chicago, the Detroit Uprising and Belle Isle, not to mention the charred embers of self-respect left behind by established groups given a live beasting by these rampaging musical brigands, MC5 were losing friends rapidly.

Thank God a killer debut album was about to drop.

Kick Out The Jams (1969)

Rob Tyner: lead vocal
Wayne Kramer: Fender guitar
Fred 'Sonic' Smith: Mosrite guitar
Michael Davis: Fender bass
Dennis Thompson: drums
John Sinclair: guidance
Brother J. C. Crawford: religious leader and spiritual advisor
Produced: Jac Holtzman, Bruce Botnick
Engineered: Bruce Botnick
Recorded live at Grande Ballroom, Detroit, 30-31 October 1968
Released: February 1969
Highest chart position: (US Billboard 200) 30

If you take everything in the universe and break it down to a common denominator, all you've got is energy – it's the level we communicate from.
Wayne Kramer, 1968

For such an exciting concert band, MC5 have been surprisingly ill-served by live albums. With a few exceptions, none since the first has paid the band proper respect, the 5's stoner rocketry shortchanged time and again by the inexpert fan with the cassette recorder, copying facilities and the buddy on the market stall. Bootleg or authorised, too many MC5 gig releases since 1972 seem to have been taped by someone a block away from the theatre, rudimentary equipment failing to capture the action as the sound waves are blown over the Detroit skyline.

With the ink barely dry on MC5's contract, Jac Holtzman was not about to compromise his shiny $20K signing with naïveté, poor atmospherics and dodgy C90 tapes. The Elektra label boss flew his go-to engineer-producer, Bruce Botnik, up from Los Angeles to oversee MC5's live debut, *Kick Out The Jams*. Botnik was one of the safest pairs of hands-on-the-faders in the business, proven by his work with West Coast-based artists such as Tim Buckley, The Doors, Love, The Beach Boys, Buffalo Springfield and The Ventures. Bruce was sold on the unusual idea of a live debut album; forget Blue Cheer; he'd never heard a louder group than the Detroiters. He reasoned that basic physics – in this case, the transfer of kinetic energy from a partisan crowd whisked to a frenzy – would surely foster an authentically exciting record. 'If we put them under studio conditions, they're just not going to perform because they need to be in front of their fans,' Botnik told the BBC in 2024. 'MC5 [was] a performing band.'

Bruce shipped in a 3M-79 1" 8-track recorder, a Universal Audio 610 console, a bunch of loudspeakers, mics and cabling and, to assist, California studio legend Wally Heider. Once the two professionals were parked in their mobile studio truck in the Grande's back alley, a CCTV camera relaying images of the gig to a small monitor, everything was in place to ensure MC5 would be suitably represented on the occasion of their maiden long player.

Botnik later asserted that he 'knew at the time we were getting a good take.' Kramer, however, would be unimpressed. With due respect to the informed opinion of the album's co-creator, the perception of any problems that beset *Kick Out The Jams* is subjective, and depends on where you stand on the classic rock 'n' roll conundrum: slavish proficiency risking sterility, or creative abandon that might deteriorate into chaos? Pre-heated by The Psychedelic Stooges, the crowd were pumped to the max by MC5's Thursday night performance. Stooge guitarist Ron Asheton echoed Wayne, though, citing the hallucinogens he claimed Thompson and Kramer had ingested before the show. 'Wayne was out of tune, and they were the sloppiest I've ever heard them in my life,' Ron told Ben Edmonds. 'Michael said his bass strings turned into giant rubber bands.'

Vigorously denying use of psychedelics on either night, Wayne insisted the 5 were intimidated by the recording equipment and the importance of the event:

I realised that it didn't sound very good. There was too much distortion and a couple of screwups, like when my string broke. I remember being terrified the night of the session. I'd borrowed a new guitar to try, and I couldn't tune it up; it wouldn't work. And Rob was fucking up. Everyone was wired up out of their gourds from the pressure.

During the set's first number, 'Ramblin' Rose', Wayne's low 'E' string slipped the bridge, throwing his guitar 'nine steps out of tune'. Mike Davis decided that missteps such as this were evidence of MC5's honesty and avoidance of antiseptic perfection. The bassist was pragmatic: 'His guitar was out of tune. Oh well, fuck it, we're MC5.'

Two weeks into November, the rough mixes brought more disappointment to the lead guitarist. On signing with Elektra, Wayne had voiced concerns the band might need more than one stab at a live debut album to get things right. Elektra allayed his worries, Holtzman promising as many more Grande nights with Bruce Botnik as necessary to ensure a satisfactory result. The label boss reneged, however. 'After running my reservations up the chain of command,' Wayne wrote, 'the consensus was to go ahead with what we had.' Sinclair, meanwhile, agreed with Davis and deferred to Holtzman, telling Jaan Uhelszki for *Uncut* in 2018:

Over the years, Wayne has made comments that he didn't like the way [*Kick Out The Jams*] turned out, but you couldn't have a more accurate representation of how the band sounded. It was bold to do a live album as a first album, but that was our aesthetic. We were a band that put on a show when nobody put on a show, except for The Who.

Whatever the roisterers in the Grande cauldron were thinking that Devil's Night, Kramer considered the show one of the 5's 'occasional train wrecks'. Was his mea culpa proof that this permanently hopped-up advocate for musical, as well as socio-political breakdown would sooner play great rock 'n' roll than parrot White Panther orthodoxy backed by 'The Red Flag' with feedback? Here, surely, was a man who took pride in his work. And the straightlaced Botnik – a man wearily familiar with the antics of Santa Monica pistoleros such as Arthur Lee, Dennis Wilson and Jim Morrison – was satisfied that MC5 individually were no more demagogic than the average fan: 'I thought they were nice guys. On stage they had the revolutionary persona, but off stage, despite the political overtones, they were like most rock bands who wanted to play music and have a good time.'

Despite Kramer's misgivings, and with a little help from an exhaustive concert schedule, *Rolling Stone*'s January cover piece, Sinclair's hustling and the notoriety born of the band's recent tribulations, MC5 were making waves beyond their home state. Released in February 1969, *Kick Out The Jams* would sell well, peaking at number 30 on *Billboard*'s top 200 albums chart. Then someone at J. L. Hudson, a popular Detroit department store and an important consumer outlet for the record industry, belatedly spotted Sinclair's colourfully unexpurgated digest of Trans-Love's credo in the album's sleevenotes. Someone else then thought it a good plan actually to listen to the album. On hearing Tyner yelling 'kick out the jams, motherfuckers' – what started as ribald barracking was now widely assumed a provocative war-cry – store managers refused to sell another copy and cancelled all subsequent orders to Elektra. Sinclair hit back with a full-page, Trans-Love branded advertisement in a local newssheet, the *Ann Arbor Argus*, headed KICK OUT THE JAMS, MOTHERFUCKER!, advice that punters should storm the doors if the shop refused them product and, in case anyone still missed the point, FUCK HUDSON'S! Sinclair also dropped in an Elektra logo and cheerily charged the ad to the record company. (John thought its placement might relieve financial woes faced by Ken Kelley, a friend of Kramer at the *Argus*, although how TLE helped Ken by neglecting to pay Hudson's a $1,600 equipment bill is anyone's guess.)

MC5 seemed to be heralding the revolution by screwing two pig-businesses at once: one which cut their discs, the other that sold them. Assuming the decision to place the ad was taken in Elektra's boardroom, Hudson's threatened to shred orders for the rest of the company's lucrative catalogue and that of its subsidiary, Nonesuch. The store was only pacified after Elektra, satisfied that no one internally had agreed this guerrilla one-off by a wayward signing, sheepishly withdrew the album's first run and hurried out a censored replacement. Rob's milder incantation for brothers and sisters to go kick out the jams was inserted per the single, which was already in the shops duly sanitised for radio play. Sinclair's original gatefold samizdat disappeared altogether.

MC5 took themselves off for a self-financed tour of the West Coast. Once the band realised the local distributor had returned his cache of now-radioactive MC5 albums to Elektra, the promotional shindig proved pointless. With no physical product to sell, the band hung out with Janis Joplin and psychotropics overlord Timothy Leary, did brief drug-related jailtime and attended Elektra's LA studios with Botnik, recording early versions of songs that would later appear on 1970's *Back In The USA*. Heading south-east, they cancelled a scheduled appearance at the Fort Lauderdale Pop Festival (arrests were in the reactionary Florida air after the *Berkeley Barb* published photos of the whole band disporting in a hotel room with a White Panther groupie) and flew back to Michigan, there to be engulfed by an even fiercer bin fire.

Faced with the choice of two versions of *Kick Out The Jams* – with or without motherfuckers, madam? – many retailers gave up on the whole idea. Radio stations relied for playlists on ratings reports, the most influential of which was a tipsheet produced by the presenter/publisher, Bill Gavin. Although the report at first predicted that the 'clean' single version of 'Kick Out The Jams' would be a massive hit – it actually peaked at number 82 on *Billboard*'s Hot 100 – Gavin's enthusiasm dried up a week later when Elektra rush-released the motherfucker-infused album. 'The rating services received reports of outraged parents calling radio stations to complain,' Wayne wrote. 'There were even reports of record store clerks being arrested for selling obscene materials. Their advice to the radio stations was to kill our record.'

Broader industry support was already draining away thanks to Laws, Graham and the promoters' cartel. Now uncertainties surrounding the album – despite sales little shy of 100,000 – conspired with Lester Bangs' ruinous April 1969 *Rolling Stone* review to swat MC5 just as they were shedding their skin. On 16 April, after a furious Jac Holtzman recoiled from Sinclair's encyclical 'to support the revolution', the Elektra boss looked over MC5's contract and hit the kill switch. Danny Fields gently reminded Holtzman that Jim Morrison – another Elektra signing, if a more profitable one – had been arrested only the previous month during a Doors concert in Miami, allegedly for flashing his dick and miming a blowjob before an audience of 15,000. The publicist was also ejected. (Danny subsequently claimed he was sacked after a separate dispute with Elektra's art director, Bill Harvey, went physical.) Fields later gave Holtzman the benefit of the doubt, positing that the more buttoned-up Elektra executives had always been gunning for MC5. 'Jac liked the idea of people with divergent tastes working for him,' Danny told Ben Edmonds, 'but there were power centres at Elektra that loathed MC5 from day one. The more conservative elements in the company wanted us gone.' At least they got to keep the leather coats.

Holtzman professed shock when he learned prominent retailers were refusing to stock the album. For John Sinclair, this reeked of betrayal, by a record company he and the band believed had their backs:

Elektra originally committed themselves to fighting any attacks on the band or the record. They convinced me to put 'motherfucker' on the record and to write whatever I wanted in the notes. So I said, Jeez, people aren't gonna like this. No, they're beyond all that, Jac told me. If there's any problems, our legal department will back you up ... Elektra just punked out on the whole thing.

So. Virginal efficiency, or dysfunctional madness? Thankfully *Kick Out The Jams* is more the latter. The album succeeds because of its mistakes, not despite them. Miles Davis was famously disdainful of New Thing and MC5's favoured jazz influences, so the great trumpeter's maxim, 'Do not fear mistakes, there are none', may feel misplaced here. But, risking the oxymoron, it's the faults that make *Kick Out The Jams* so perfect. Rock 'n' roll *should* be dirty and dangerous, rank with discordant impurities. Sometimes so fast and frantic it risks careening into the buffers, or so slow and steady it gels like blood in a thrombotic artery, it was never meant to have the roughness smoothed off. In its ragged, greasy, grimy glory, *Kick Out The Jams* dives deepest of all four official MC5 albums (including the much later *Heavy Lifting*) into the molten iron core of avant-rock. The next record would be closer to the purist, anything-long-enough-is-too-long rock 'n' roll ideal that would drive punk, the third an uncertain but largely enjoyable combination of the two. But for now, MC5 were amping and psychedelicising everything off the meter – just because they could.

Wayne was as nonplussed by the sleeve of *Kick Out The Jams* as he was the record's sonics. Although he had approved Gary Grimshaw's 'ingenious and dramatic' mockups, the final cover would look nothing like them. A collage supposedly representing the blissful bacchanale of Zenta New Year at the Grande was more like the hangover after the riot at the DNC. Elektra's risk-averse lawyers, dreading hundreds of cease-and-desist letters from litigious parents, instructed the art department to replace montaged audience photos with anonymous, airbrushed renderings. Glory shots of Rob Tyner made much of the singer's gap teeth and pasty complexion, Dennis Thompson appeared to be poking a drumstick up his nose and Elektra's head of art Bill Harvey included a little extra pic on the front in the top right-hand corner. Of himself.

'Ramblin' Rose' 2.39 (Marijohn Wilkin, Fred B. Burch)

Brothers and sisters, I wanna see a sea of hands out there
Let me see a sea of hands
I want everybody to kick up some noise
I wanna hear some revolution out there, brothers
I wanna hear a little revolution
Brothers and sisters, the time has come for each and every one of you to decide whether you are gonna be the problem or whether you are gonna be the solution (that's right)

You must choose, brothers, you must choose
It takes five seconds, five seconds of decision
Five seconds to realise your purpose here on the planet
It takes five seconds to realise that it's time to move
It's time to get down with it, brothers, it's time to testify and I want to know
Are you ready to testify? Are you ready?
I give you a testimonial:
The MC5!

No sooner were blessings bestowed upon the Grande believers by Brother J. C. Crawford – the Oracle Remus, as the band knew him – and MC5 were colliding into the opening bars of their debut album like neutrons at Three Mile Island. Even those of us suckled on the carnage of The Who at their most belligerent were unprepared for such an onslaught.

First recorded by Jerry Lee 'The Killer' Lewis in 1961, 'Ramblin' Rose' was co-written by Marijohn Wilkin, who composed sweet Nashville country and rockabilly hits such as 'Cut Across Shorty', 'Long Black Veil' and, with Kris Kristofferson, the religious chestnut 'One Day At A Time'. Since Wilkin died in 2006, the devout songsmith had plenty of time to seeth over – and, one would pray, offer absolution for – MC5's unhallowed disassembly of her earlier song, albeit one Marijohn had penned several years before she and God found each other in the 1970s.

The Sun Records hit by Jerry Lee Lewis – the deeply flawed but brilliant Louisiana rocker was himself no stranger to devotional fervour, befitting a southern Baptist who married his thirteen year old first cousin and shot his bassist thinking the man was a Coke bottle – was sax-driven, thinly-disguised sexual innuendo. Now MC5 were pumping the song full of hormones and putting out it to a whole new market.

Disappointed Wayne Kramer may have been, but if his carelessly mislaid E-string eight bars in is detectable only to witnesses or a tutored ear, to everyone else it's part of the overall gaiety. 'Ramblin' Rose' is The Killer's original maxxed-out as a lascivious, sex-drenched come-on, pulverised by guitars that seemed to be wrangling a stallion with acid in its feed. A relatively short intro to the album, the song is oddly showbizzy: with Rob Tyner's entrance delayed, likely due less to tardiness or drugs than to the 5's strategy of milking an expectantly feverish audience, understudy Kramer breaks in and out of the tsunami of amplified sound in a hoarse, falsetto croak. Thompson's drumming is all over the place, but where another band would have cashiered him at the audition, maybe even enticed the more conventionally proficient Bob Gaspar back from the bank job, Dennis's intensity and commitment add further layers to the sonic disorder on which MC5 roll. It's a great intro, crashing to a close as the whooping from everyone in the room sets up one of the great moments in rock. Marijohn Wilkin must have been thrilled.

'Kick Out The Jams' 2.37 (MC5)

There are signature tunes, and there are pieces so closely bound to an artist the ties are umbilical. Just as the song was birthed by MC5, the band was made by the song. In 2018, Wayne told Jaan Uhelszki of *Uncut* how he and Rob had occupied the kitchen of the Trans-Love commune to write, one of which results was 'Kick Out The Jams'. The pair knew they'd nailed the band's worldview long before the tune became shorthand for rock 'n' roll infamy:

> I had a little amp and we would sit there and I'd throw riffs at Rob and chord changes, and he would usually have a couplet or two of lyrics and we'd just try to fit them together. We just tried to knock something out pretty quickly. Tyner … was telling us, 'Don't try and change me, let me be who I am.' He was framing it like the story of what happened on a night when we played. We all got in tune. When the dressing room got hazy, it got hazy with reefer smoke. And then we got crazy.

Tyner rarely did things by halves. As a writer and thinker he was smart as a whip, boasting the intellectual chops to mount an eloquent defence of John Sinclair's takeaway Situationism even as he acknowledged its deficiencies. As a performer, he was at once singer, sherpa, showman and shaman, his flair for theatrics rivalling that of Jim Morrison. For one concert finale, Rob was 'shot' onstage, his colleagues' guitars replaced by deactivated rifles. Occasionally, roadie Steve Harnadek would appear from the wings brandishing a starting pistol, a sharp crack sending Tyner to the floor, mirroring labelmate Morrison's concurrent melodramatics in The Doors' 'The Unknown Soldier'. With outros like that, it was hardly surprising that Tyner's intro appearance, one song in, became a regular, crowd-pleasing set-piece, and an integral part of MC5's performance.

The Grande by now in a tizz, the full band firing on all twelve, Rob grabs the mic and issues rock 'n' roll's most misunderstood battlecry. The equally famous riff kicks in, then within a few lines whatever 'revolutionary' artifice MC5 have, willingly or not, projected as their raison d'etre is burned off in pre-coital abandon:

> Well, I feel pretty good and I guess that I could get crazy now, baby
> 'Cause we all got in tune and when the dressing room got hazy, now baby
> I know how you want it child, hot, quick and tight
> The girls can't stand it when you're doin' it right
> Let me up on the stand and let me kick out the jams
> Yeah, kick out the jams, I wanna kick 'em out.

Later in the song the words reference a Miss McKenzie, a fictional inspiration whose name, as Wayne advised Uhelszki, 'just rhymed good with leaping frenzy'. He explained why, like The Doors, MC5 had credited all original songs on the first album to the band instead of individual writers. 'We were communists,' he said, somewhat disingenuously. 'It's a way to keep a band together.' How things would change.

At last count, 'Kick Out The Jams' has been covered at least thirty times, with Tyner's one-liner alone sampled by some twenty artists. 'I think the reason the song lives on is because it seems to sum up that slightly over-the-top enthusiasm that youth have,' Wayne offered, adding, in a sly dig at MC5's bogeyman Lester Bangs, '[Like] nineteen year old punks on a meth power trip.'

To mark its 40th anniversary in April 2009, the song was reissued as a vinyl 7-inch single in America, peaking at number 39 on *Billboard*. Spotify marked the event by including 'Kick Out The Jams' on a one-off playlist, alarmingly labelled by the streaming service, 'Uplifting Songs of Motivation'. The first few uplifting, motivational moments from the original were politely excised. Anyone expecting a Marijohn Wilkin compilation could breathe easy.

'Come Together' 4.17 (MC5)

The album's third track takes a clear lead from 'I Can See For Miles'. Written by Tyner and Smith, 'Come Together' has been cited as conclusive evidence MC5 were only soundalikes feeding on the electrical impulses left behind by The Who. While the similarities between the songs are self-evident, however, few today would slam the 5 for plagiarism. To do so would be to question most hard rock played since 1965, whether it identifies as punk, grunge, Britpop, heavy/speed/black/thrash/Norwegian death metal or any other overexuberant media invention. The Who influenced MC5, the 5 in turn inspired The New York Dolls, who begat 1976 Britpunk, which led to 1987 grunge, which ... you know where this goes. Like haircuts and sensible shoes, fashion in pop music shifts from one generation to the next. Journalists, marketers, socio/political conditions, sometimes even the musicians themselves: all oversee how rock is structured, whether it seeks broad commercial success or cultish exclusivity. When an art form is meant to be experienced in the moment – particularly one as cyclical and derivative of itself as rock 'n' roll – the inevitable sense of déjà vu ceases to matter. If it didn't, we'd all still be living in 1957, or wearing mullets.

'Come Together' is the erectile zenith of *Kick Out The Jams* and this author's favourite MC5 tune (along with 'Looking At You'). The metallic effect of this astonishing track is intensified by the feedback, excreted from the playing as if by electronic leeches. Critics in 1969 saw this as verifying MC5's musical shortcomings, but such a reductive argument missed the point as surely as Tera Shirma's engineers in 1966 and, at least for a while, Lester Bangs. The 5 intended every last epilepsy-inducing howl. A massive dopamine hit of MC5 at their most primal, 'Come Together' is also a ringside seat to cocksman Tyner getting it on:

All the guiding rhythms lover, all the nerve that take a lover
Nipples stiffen, nipples stiffen, nipples stiffen, mama
Let me give tongue to it, yes, let me give tongue to it, yes, ah
Together in the darkness, come with me, oh
Yes, yes, yes, together mama, yes, yes, yes, yes, yes, yes, yes, yes, wow.

Yes, wow. No storming the establishment's last bastion just yet, then, at least not before the post-coital cigarette. Instead, singer and band give graphic voice to the most engorged bout of musical poontang since Casanova swiped right on the Happy Hooker's Tinder app. At 1.13 Wayne pokes out a brief solo, but it's all but smothered, a slave to the rhythm method. Rarely has pure sex been so lubriciously celebrated in song. It bypassed many at the time, but perhaps everyone was too busy rooting around under the Hill House floorboards for the seditious literature to notice what MC5 were really all about. Jane Birkin and Serge Gainsbourg, eat your hearts out.

'Rocket Reducer No.62 (Rama Lama Fa Fa Fa)' 5.01 (MC5)
Gil Scott-Heron got it wrong: the revolution *will* be televised, but only after the 9pm watershed. Especially if the soundtrack is a song that combines the unexpurgated urgency of MC5 at full throttle with the joys of sex and sniffing glue.

The titular reducer was an industrial solvent, rocket-propelled according to its makers, so abrasive it stripped paint from an engine block and receptors from the nervous system of any thrillseeker ignoring the fine print on the can. Such impetuous adventurers included MC5: 'Party, party, party,' wrote Mike Davis for the sleevenote of the 2008 compilation album *Motorcity Rebels*. 'I wouldn't advise trying Rocket Reducer No.62. It's a toxic substance and it can kill you. What were we thinking?'

Indeed. With Tyner's refactory period normalised following 'Come Together', his bandmates are jacked into a beta state of frenzied, dope-fuelled hyperactivity. 'Rocket Reducer No.62 (Rama Lama Fa Fa Fa)' is last in the devastating quartet that comprises side one of *Kick Out The Jams*. Rob intros the song with a septum-puncturing coke sneeze or a Donald Duck impression – you choose – before the band set up a galloping rhythm, finding their feet after a few bars as Wayne shows off his left-hand hammering technique. Another squall of feedback, plenty of vocally clamoured 'heys', 'right nows' and 'rama-lamas', and we're off to the races, with a song that was already a concussive centrepiece of the 5's live act. Thompson hammers away, apparently in half a dozen different and not necessarily compatible time signatures, although in the context of MC5 (and likely no one else) it works. Kramer and Smith slice at the bedlam like fencers with chainsaws, while Tyner summarises the only principles of the WPP manifesto MC5 could really be arsed with. His words exude yet more unblushingly sexist braggadocio:

Workin' here before your momma/Soakin' wet
You think you're satisfied/You ain't seen nothing yet
I said wham bam thank you ma'am
I'm a born ass pincher/And I don't give a damn
Rama lama fa fa fa ...

Misogyny had been part of the lingua franca of rock 'n' roll and the blues since a woman first done Lightnin' Hopkins wrong and he reached for his shotgun. By 1968, as the hip disciples spread the good news of workers' unity and the coming unshackling, the tradwives were still sidelined; holding up not the sky, as Mao Zedong imagined, but the shelf where the dusters were kept. It was a man's job, eating the rich, especially with costumes to stitch. 'We were sexist bastards,' Kramer admitted to Legs McNeil and Gillian McCain for *Please Kill Me: The Uncensored Oral History Of Punk.* 'We were not politically correct at all.' As Ann Arbor activist Sam Treacy remarked to Iggy Pop's biographer, Joe Ambrose, 'There was an awful lot of house cleaning and meal preparation going on.' Not to mention sewing sequins onto spangly tops.

No acreage of stage glitz, of course, will deter conservatives from rejecting all lefties as unsmiling puritans, too straightjacketed by denial and hair-shirt preaching to let rip and enjoy life. But while Trans-Love was anxious to preserve the urban-guerrilla notoriety – a pose Bernie Rhodes would one day craft into a compelling visual brand for The Clash – any idea of MC5 as dour Khmer Rouge workcamp minders imposing Year Zero on the sod-tilling popular masses was pushing it. This was one cadre of oversexed alpha males that was gonna have fun; all the chicks had to do was to lie back and enjoy it. And if anyone challenged this male prerogative – well, kick out the jams, motherfuckers.

'Borderline' 2.45 (MC5)

'Borderline' is the live version of the studio song that backed the second MC5 single, 'Looking At You'. It feels like a comedown after the heavy lifting on side one, the brilliance of *Kick Out The Jams'* first four tracks mildly compromised by the second. Although there are good moments, by comparison the rest of the record falters, as if the 5's dealer was busted just as someone got up to turn over the record, leaving Brothers Wayne, Fred, Rob, Mike and Dennis shivering and jonesing to cop.

Kramer conceded their live set of the time was top-heavy, the most exciting moments often already done before the end of the show: 'We front-loaded the set list,' he wrote. 'We came on full bore, and left ourselves no headroom. Dialling it back was a level of sophistication we hadn't achieved yet. It made us great and limited at the same time.' If 'Borderline' was another bullet-point on Wayne's lengthening charge-sheet against *Kick Out The Jams*, for Mike Davis the song was an overlooked favourite: 'I wanted to play it in London [in 2003, for an MC5 partial reunion], but no one else would even consider it.'

'Borderline' was written by Kramer and Davis when they shared a rooming house in 1966. 'One day Wayne came up to show me a new song he was working on,' Mike wrote. 'All he had was a rudimentary guitar riff. I said, that's great, it's so raw. So we sat and I played my bass along with the simple little part.' Davis reckoned 'Borderline' represented 'power of the most basic type', and potentially he's not far wrong. With preambling audience hubbub removed in the service of startling the listener into side two, the 5 crash the opening bars like an accident in a steelyard, before Wayne drills through the metal and a song takes shape. Unfortunately the promising intro degrades to a stutter. Instead of allowing the early momentum to build a proper head of steam, the musicians stop and start uncertainly, as if Wayne and Mike are still jamming back in their digs.

When the pair played their demo to Smith, Tyner and Thompson, Sonic put together the middle 3/4 time breaks while Rob fashioned a lyric that Davis freely admitted he found ambiguous. 'I think [the song] gets lost because no one can understand what the lyrics mean,' Mike wrote. 'In a weird way, I do. It's about being passionate and confused at the same time.' So it is, as Tyner grapples with what may be his earliest sexual congress – he's not yet the babe-magnet of 'Come Together' – and frets that his partner's lissom moves might bring him too close to the 'Borderline': the event horizon at the brink of his premature wipeout:

Need you girl, can't you feel/I just got to know, if it's real
Big and strong, hard and fine
But you're movin' around, pushin' me past
My borderline, yeah yeah.

Mike felt the song would have benefited by addressing 'something more macho'. It's difficult to ascribe anything other than bristling adolescent testosterone to the lyrics, even if they do address a natural sexual nervousness. But as the bassist concluded, 'it is like it is.'

'Motor City Is Burning' 4.30 (Al Smith)

Just when we thought it was safe to return to the frontline, Brother Crawford springs up like Zebedee tweaking on sulphate to remind his flock that they, not 'a lot of honkies sitting on a lot of money', are 'the high society'. Adding to the Black Panthers' misgivings over the WPP project, Jesse's final benediction, between 'Borderline' and 'Motor City Is Burning', would only be outdone for wiggah condescension a month or so later by Grace Slick, when Airplane's singer plastered her face with black makeup and waved her fist in the air for the Smothers Brothers' TV show.

Less Michigan than Mississippi Delta, and the only song on the album that might loosely be described as political – although hardly the summons to the siege-engines Sinclair might have wanted – 'Motor City Is Burning' is a blues, a genre the 5 had almost bent out of shape by 1968, composed not by the band but by Al B. Smith. The Vee-Jay Records' executive wrote the song for John Lee Hooker – the legendary bluesman apparently claimed the composition as his own – after the Detroit riots of 1967, part of which conflagration Hooker witnessed from his home on Jameson Street. As interpreted by MC5, the song feels like a soundcheck; a ponderous and unexceptional twelve-bar, bringing down the averages on the convulsive wallop hitherto radiated by the band. Tyner upgrades Smith/Hooker's original lyrics for topicality, evoking Black Panther snipers, the National Guard, pigs in the streets and the acrid miasma of the unrest. Nine years later, 'Motor City Is Burning' would inspire another slice of vicarious rabble-rousing, 'London's Burning', from The Clash's eponymous debut album.

'I Want You Right Now' 6.02 (Colin Frechter, Larry Page)
Despite Lester Bangs not getting MC5 (until he did), the renowned controversialist's Troggs comparison made sense. 'I Want You Right Now' is the 5's beefed-up, slowed-down version of a boneheadedly simple ditty the bumpkins coupled with their 1966 hit single 'With A Girl Like You', and it's as heavy as MC5 get. Essentially 'Wild Thing' on Quaaludes, 'I Want You' (the 'Right Now' was added by Elektra's typographer, mistaking the Grande crowd's spirited yelping for part of the title) begins with Wayne sliding up and down his fretboard, issuing four painfully distorted, Townshend-like chords that shoot out of the speakers like crossbow bolts. On the fourth, the band crash into the song, the famous theme penetrative enough to crumble the Grande's venerable bricks to sand.

The song is three chords and a huge riff, punctuated by Rob hoarsely declaiming a lyric that never reaches beyond another gasping statement of sexual desire. After two minutes, taken back to a lone Davis slowly strumming his bass to Tyner's soulman testifying, the buildup to the finale is an inevitably massive return to The Troggs, but by now as blocked as a Who roadie at the Fillmore. Unashamedly pre-loved, the same grade of punk-metal The Clash were pleased to recast ten years later for their excellent second album *Give 'Em Enough Rope*, 'I Want You' likely provoked the most vocal disapproval MC5 were obliged to endure. A replica, then – but a latheringly, exuberantly, cretinously exciting one.

'Starship' 8.26 (MC5, Sun Ra)
The album's final track was not the original Devil's Night finale. That honour fell, as usual, to 'Black To Comm'. However, the quality on both nights of the wild two-chord epic was not deemed good enough for an album release. As Tyner told Ben Edmonds:

We didn't think ['Black To Comm'] worked those evenings. That was the experimental nature of the time. If something relies on magic to happen, sometimes the magic happens and sometimes it doesn't, and you can't force it, and there's no substitute for it.

The album's lighters-in-the-air moment fell instead to a lengthy jam based loosely on one of Sun Ra's poems. Any notion these pop-star layabouts should have the cojones to evoke, as presumed co-composer, the high priest of the cosmic avant-garde and one of the most respected bandleaders on the planet – planet Saturn, that is – might have given the free-jazz fraternity beyond Detroit collective pause for derision. But the 5 were now travelling light years from any semblance of rock music as we knew it. Given Sinclair's keenness to pow-wow with the Black Panthers, and fellow jazz nuts Tyner, Kramer and Davis' goal of marrying the raging, atonal voice of African-American protest to the 5's own frightening but still comparatively standard oeuvre, connubial bliss between theoretically disparate genres seemed assured. Besides, a credit for Sun Ra would surely earn the great Afrofuturist's estate richly-deserved royalties once this world caught up with MC5 – not to mention Ra – and bought the album by the million.

Everything's relative: the ultra-high-powered and frenetic MC5 were to on-brand rock groups what the 5's favourite alt-jazzers were to Maynard Ferguson and Stan Kenton. Unlike, say, brass-rockers Chicago or Blood, Sweat & Tears, MC5 would have frightened away such eminences by several time zones, but the new jazz could be disordered enough to feed into the 5's own sense of audial entropy without showing the join.

'Starship' begins conventionally enough – or as ordinarily as the 5 deign to get – as Rob calls the tune over an oscillating wave of guitar feedback and Dennis's rapid-fire kick drums:

Starship, starship take me/Take me where I want to go
Out there among the planets/Let a billion suns cast my shadow
Starship, starship take me/Stretch our legs in time and space
Take a passage through the vacuum/Let me feel the stars burnin' on my face.

Rob follows the first two verses by counting down a checklist that could have been straight out of the 1960s telly animation *Space Patrol*; 'Ten for the gravity, checkpoint ... nine for polarity, checkpoint ... yobba rays on ...' etc. Wayne and Sonic scrub frantically, their massive block chords gushing feedback, while Machine Gun pilots in a lunar module only to have it flatten his drum riser. Tyner announces that we're all leaving the solar system, then at 1.53 everything pulls up short, as if the starship has run into a Klingon warbird and come second.

From here until the end of the song, it's Sun Ra all the way – or, perhaps, MC5's take on the sulphurous instability the Myth-Science Arkestra sometimes unleashed. The band toggle between spooky, echoey, oddly Floydian soundscaping and atmospheric use of space – the musical variety – while each musician relocates to a different corner of the galaxy and cranks up to eleven. It's cacophonous, an extreme musical-emotional stress test, and quite hard work in places. But then, Herman Poole 'Sun Ra' Blount was rarely known for his melodic delicacy whenever he donned his glittery free-jazz space bonnet. Why should MC5 be any different?

Once the cosmic chaos has equalised, strangely the 5 don't circle back to their default pedal-to-the-metal crunch for a brain-blasting final few bars. Instead 'Starship' fizzles out as if the dilithium crystals have suddenly packed up. The band – and, it must be said, the listener – are marooned 2,000 light years from home, with not a relief shuttle in sight.

Despite Tyner's reservations, 'Black To Comm' likely saw in the Zenta New Year very nicely after 'Starship'. But the effect of the 5 apparently taking their foot off the gas following the magnificent first (vinyl) side of *Kick Out The Jams* is counter-intuitive and strangely deflating. Still, predictability was never what MC5 were about.

'Starship' was covered – if losing four minutes, the vocal and most of the Ra-centric audioscaping qualified as a cover – by Spacemen 3 for *Transparent Radiation*, the British shoegaze band's 1987 EP.

Back In The USA (1970)

Personnel:
Rob Tyner: lead vocal
Wayne Kramer: guitar (solos on 'Tutti-Frutti', 'Teenage Lust', 'Looking At You', 1st & 3rd choruses of 'Back In The USA')
Fred 'Sonic' Smith: guitar (solos on 'The American Ruse', 2nd chorus of 'Back In The USA'), lead vocal ('Shakin' Street')
Michael Davis: bass
Dennis Thompson: drums
Danny Jordan: keyboards
Produced: Jon Landau
Engineered: Jim Bruzzese
Recorded at GM Studios, East Detroit
Released: January 1970
Highest chart position: (US Billboard 200) 137; (UK Official Albums Chart) 74

> Our souls got psychedelicized there for a while, so it felt good to be back in the pocket.
> Rob Tyner

Three or four studio albums are normally tucked away before a rock band has the confidence to commit a live concert to posterity. Given the stampeding authority of *Kick Out The Jams*, and the risk that MC5's recorded output could prove to be as top-heavy as early individual shows (see Wayne Kramer's concerns above), fans and critics were wise to contain their excitement ahead of the second LP. Those craving more of the same now wondered if the 5 had, weirdly, become their own bill-toppers. After the first record's exposition of MC5-power, what calibre of musical howitzer could continue to bust apart the competition? Were the 5 about to start yelling 'kick out the jams' at themselves?

The reception given *Back In The USA* suggests expectations were severely mismanaged, not least by some members of MC5. The raw materials were there. Five years of relentless gigging had realised a flawed but brilliant debut. MC5's confidence and attack were present and murderously correct. Months of being poked, prodded, billyclubbed and bullshitted had rubbed the band up so badly the steam-heated aggression had only one outlet short of actual physical violence. And the new material was stupendous: a bunch of great original songs, bookended by a brace of classics on which MC5 paid worshipful respect to two of their heroes. So what happened?

Jon Landau happened, is the popular answer, for better or for worse. Brooklyn-born and Boston-based, the journalist described by Danny Fields as 'the single most influential person in America on the rock scene' had been blown away by MC5's spirit and verve, if not their technical prowess. Clearly no respecter of editorial detachment, even while writing for such inviolable texts as *Rolling Stone* and *Crawdaddy*, effectively Jon became Elektra's consultant analyst, penning a 30-page treatise on the 5's strengths and weaknesses that would gladden the heart of any management consultant. The Elektra contract was already inked, if not long of this earth, so it's uncertain what such scrutiny would have achieved. However, Landau's support for MC5 would open doors. And lo, did *Rolling Stone* editor and Landau's boss, Jann Wenner, dispatch young Eric Ehrmann to spawn that five-page MC5 teen-piece even before *Kick Out The Jams* was causing Hudson's purchasing department a collective fit of the vapours.

MC5 and Sinclair sounded out producers. Landau's studio experience was as untested as the 5's, but he had a deep knowledge of, and love for the music. He also maintained a bulging Rolodex of rockbiz heavyweights, among them Atlantic Records' vice-president, Jerry Wexler. Though Sinclair was about to be neutered, the Trans-Love leader was persuaded that Landau should oversee the 5's second LP, despite early talks with J. Geils Band producers Brad Shapiro and Dave Crawford. Sinclair also hoped the journalist's industry clout would placate those who had dissed MC5 as poseurs, plagiarists and pariahs. Cool about Landau's inexperience, he told Ben Edmonds: 'The critics think MC5 is a hype and that we're just a garage band, so to win them over, on the next album we'll use one of their own. [Landau] had studied the group from a production point of view, and I thought it would be a stroke of genius to use him.'

After years steeped in jazz and R&B, Atlantic Records had begun mining a rich seam of popular electric rock. Geils, Cream, Buffalo Springfield, Led Zeppelin, Iron Butterfly, Yes and Crosby, Stills & Nash were among recent signings. With Elektra and the 5 on the brink of divorce, Sinclair nudged Landau into teasing Wexler: could the great man's organisation succeed with the fractious Detroiters where Atlantic's rivals had lucked out? A fortnight after Elektra signed the decree absolute, Sinclair and Fields huddled with Wexler. The Atlantic VP bit, agreeing a contract that gave MC5 complete creative control and a cash advance of $50,000. Jon, not Jerry, would produce; having cut discs for Aretha Franklin, King Curtis, Ray Charles and other jazz and R&B glitterati, Wexler thought most rock music was crap, no matter its profitability. Advised by David Newman, an accountant tasked by Fields with unravelling the 5's shambolic finances, the band settled their bills and took a six-bedroom farmhouse in rural Hamburg, Michigan, consciously distancing themselves from the TLE-WPP freakshow. 'Hill Street had become impractical,' Kramer wrote, tactfully. Landau moved into the house, while each bandmate celebrated his rejuvenated good fortune with a new ride: a station wagon for family man Rob (he'd married Becky in 1968), Corvettes for Fred and Dennis and a Buick Riviera for Mike. Only Wayne snubbed both the Motor City and America, choosing a plum-coloured, '63 model Jaguar XK-E.

The '68 model MC5 would have reddened at the keep-fit regime Landau now imposed on his out-of-shape clients. Gone – theoretically – were excessive booze, reefer, acid and solvent; in came running, callisthenics, barbells and yoghurt. 'We went on the protein-only diet,' remembered Michael Davis:

> Steak, cottage cheese, salad, eggs and eight glasses of water per day were the limits of our sustenance. We must have substituted whiskey for beer too, because I can't imagine us not drinking. Rob was also required to jog around the house 50 times every day. After just two weeks, I felt incredibly weak from lack of a balanced diet, and promptly mutinied.

Landau intended his fitness drive for the music, too. Never convinced by MC5's expressionist-psychedelic tendencies, he adored the no-frills r'n'r basics he knew they could nail in their sleep. Everything would now be so polished you could use it for shaving, as ripped as the newly-fit gym rats themselves: eleven songs, nine under three minutes in length, just one over four, with nary a fire-in-the-pet-shop, free-jazz extravagance within the album's spartan 28 minutes.

Elektra refused to release the masters of the songs recorded with Bruce Botnik in LA: 'Teenage Lust', 'The Human Being Lawnmower' and 'Call Me Animal'. Atlantic stepped up and paid Holtzman $10,000 for the rights, and time was booked at East Detroit's G. M. Studios. Offering only a four-track machine, owner Guido Marasco promised an eight-track once MC5 had settled their first bill. Marasco's partner, Jim Bruzzese, a skilled audio engineer and former big-band drummer, would join Landau at the desk.

On 25 July 1969, the two spliffs John Sinclair had unwittingly shared with an undercover policewoman two years before returned to burn him badly. A trial jury found him guilty of possession and Judge Robert J. Colombo handed down nine and a half to ten years' imprisonment. His Honor, a hardliner who didn't like hippies, denied bond. For MC5 as well as their hapless manager, the incarceration was a watershed. Prior to trial, as attorneys predicted custodial doom, the band moved for an amicable split. In departing, the 5 made an open-ended pledge to support Sinclair's family and pay legal defence costs. John took his firing badly. 'It was as if he was blaming his bust on me and the band,' Wayne wrote, 'then punishing us for trying to help.' Beginning to regret championing the new producer, Sinclair believed the real culprit was Landau, who had quietly suggested MC5 'get rid of all these freeloaders' – meaning all three rings of the Trans-Love/White Panthers/Zenta circus. Sinclair also railed against Jon's efforts to elbow away 'naïve and unprofessional' political posturing.

Although MC5 generously promised TLE twenty per cent of the band's gross income, an embittered Sinclair wrote from the slammer to *Rolling Stone* claiming he'd not seen a penny from the 5 since going away. He also insisted that Trans-Love had financially buttressed the band for years. Kramer countered that earnings had been funnelled into a central account to pay bills, adding that MC5 themselves had made little. '[We] never had any money and never had any personal possessions,' Wayne said, leather coats and XK-Es clearly mere business expenses. A proffered olive branch failed to staunch the bad blood, as he told *Rolling Stone*:

> I wrote [Sinclair] to explain my feelings, and we had to make some kind of arrangements for the future. He wrote me back a paranoid rant. He says, 'You guys wanted to be bigger than The Beatles, and I wanted you to be bigger than Chairman Mao'.

By August 1969, the severity of Sinclair's 'ten for two' penalty had become another countercultural cause célèbre. Among those picking up the cry, come on down Abbie Hoffman, now one of seven with legal jeopardies of their own following the DNC. A month after Sinclair was jailed, Abbie travelled to the Woodstock Music & Arts Fair, there to find a convenient moment to pontificate before the cornered half-million. Instead of interrupting Jefferson Airplane, Country Joe, CSNY or any other of the festival's more right-on contributors, the activist mysteriously elected The Who, appropriating a mic just as the ex-mods were barrelling through Pete Townshend's cherished *Tommy*. Egged on by a very stoned Pun Plamondon, the interloper vented over Brother John's appalling treatment at the hands of The Man: 'I think this is a pile of shit while John Sinclair rots in prison,' Hoffman boomed, his perceptions by now severely battered by microdot. Townshend, likely in no better condition, swung his Gibson SG. Moments later Abbie was picking himself out of the photographers' pit.

MC5 discussed management options with Landau and Fields. The pair recommended Dee Anthony, an associate of influential booking agent Frank Barsalona. An archetypally conservative recordbiz bruiser – and almost certainly unsuited to corralling rebellious young dissolutes like MC5 – Bronx-born Anthony at least came with a pedigree; he currently minded US interests for numerous successful British bands, including Jethro Tull, Traffic and Ten Years After. But Dennis Thompson detected Mob leanings. When MC5's accountant magically found no money to pay tax, rumours of Anthony's connections gathered pace. There followed an awkward period of semi-management, enlivened by Dee's fireside tales of showbiz ribaldry with former client Tony Bennett. Anthony went dark and the agreement was annulled. Later, Anthony sued the 5 for allegedly welshing on commissions and expenses. Estimating MC5 were in the hole for $40,000, Dennis gamely took over management for eight months using his father's credit card.

Studio sessions for the second album were underway, flawlessness the objective. Lester Bangs' takedown of *Kick Out The Jams* still hurt, but Kramer and Landau were in lockstep, establishing a chain of command with which the others, easily as outspoken but less well-organised, could only comply. With Michael's rubber bass strings and his own dropped E still resonating,

Wayne was leaving nothing to chance. 'The tempos are going to be right,' he told Edmonds. 'No excuses for anything to go wrong. It was like a make it or break it. Our local popularity had peaked, and we needed to make a strong statement on a national and international level.'

Landau wanted to rein in Thompson's busier instincts. 'My role model for a drummer was early Charlie Watts or the Stax drummer Al Jackson,' he said. '[On] The Rolling Stones' version of 'Can I Get A Witness', the groove is incredible, and Charlie does not play one single fill.' Thompson wasn't happy. Obliged to work to an unfamiliar click track, at one point he dismissed Landau as 'a fascist dictator', although later he softened. Mike Davis's memoir acknowledged the bassman's own musical shortcomings: 'They were isolating my bass track, so all that played back were naked bass notes. I'd only been playing for a few years, and it was painful to listen to the fumbling and jerking.'

Davis claimed to have contributed to four tracks, but Landau insisted otherwise. Despite the brief Hamburg health kick, the producer hinted of damage wrought by Mike's emergent heroin habit: 'Michael is not on the record. He was just not in shape to deliver the necessary discipline.' Wayne sniffed: '[Mike] had never learned to play the bass within the traditional musical constructs of harmony, tempo, timing and consistency.' Landau proposed a gun for hire, Jerry Jemmott, but the band preferred to keep everything in the family. 'After a few sessions,' Jon continued, 'I finally had to say, Wayne, you're playing bass.' Kramer was down with this, but both he and his producer lacked the experience of a seasoned studio pro such as Jemmott. He told David Fricke for tidal.com:

We listened to everything at such volume that it all sounded great. It wasn't until the record was released that I started getting feedback: 'it all sounds a little thin'. I didn't know how to set up the gear, how to EQ the bass tones. And Landau had no experience recording rock bands. It was the blind leading the blind.

Dennis believed the true punk ethic was notable for its absence. Far from unchaining the lusty brio that was MC5's brand, Landau's absolutism ate the record's soul. '*Back In The USA* exemplified everything we weren't because it was trying to be so perfect,' Dennis said. 'It would have been better if we dropped a beat here or there and focused on capturing the energy, even if that meant a bad note in the solo.'

For all the concerns of band, producer, critics and fans, however, *Back In The USA* would one day be deified as punk's foundational text, particularly in Britain. For this was rock 'n' roll Redux, more spit than polish. Jon Landau might have intended the album to sound like it was cut at Chess Records in 1958, a return to the music that had gotten everyone up in the morning since 'Johnny B. Goode' was first played under the bedsheets, but MC5 made damn sure of a modernist reboot. At its best, the album proves how well the 5 learned to weaponise simplicity, the twisted, monstrously heavy urban blues and unchained avant-jazz of *Kick Out The Jams* now blowtorched back to the primer, even as the energy levels soar.

It's true that in places, notably the non-originals, the frequency equalisation is so hot, bare and flat that MC5 seemed to risk evisceration, as if a more cynical producer had performed keyhole surgery in an attempt to laser out any lingeringly malignant cells of pure rock 'n' roll. Yet as 'Tutti-Frutti' segues to 'Tonight' and 'The Human Being Lawnmower' hands over to 'Back In The USA', the joins are audible, even jarring, suggesting Landau deliberately allowed the floor to fall out of the two classics while ensuring MC5's own songs were relatively copper-bottomed. The album is nowhere near as viscous and weighty as its predecessor; but taken loud enough to drain the cochlea, bass pumped to bursting, *Back In The USA* is as thrillingly visceral as you could want from MC5: a band now proving, beyond doubt, they could capture the essence of original rock 'n' roll without fetishising its primitivism.

The material was probably never bettered by MC5: crisp, memorable sketches of cars and girls, hormones and high-school hops, the safe spaces for urban youth where parents, police and politicians feared to tread. Classic American Midwest rock 'n' roll, then. Kramer told Fricke how he and Tyner used to write in their kitchen, stoked by plenty of weed: 'We'd smoke joints; I would play guitar; Rob would listen. He had a notepad on his knee. I'd play something, and he'd say, 'Wait a minute, play that again.' We wrote most of the songs on *Kick Out The Jams* and *Back In The USA* that way.'

Although no reviewer matched Bangs' venomous attack on the first album, critical response to *Back In The USA* was mixed. In *Rolling Stone*, Greil Marcus applauded the record's 'attempt to define themes and problems and [find] political, social, and emotional solutions'. However, 'the care with which these themes have been shaped drags it down'. At first sceptical, Robert 'The Dean' Christgau was won over: 'Under Jon Landau, the 5's style has become choppier, harder, and more concise; when his discipline is imposed on the soaring Sinclair-meets-Coltrane expansionism of their Elektra album, as on 'Looking At You', the tension is pyrotechnic'. Writing for *Allmusic* in 2015, Jason Ankeny took the belatedly popular line: the second album is 'in many regards MC5's best and most influential.' And in his 2018 interview with Kramer, radio jock Jim Kerr remembered his early days deejaying in Ann Arbor: 'We played the hell out of [*Back In The USA*] ... that album was very finely crafted. Sonically, it holds up today.'

Relatively few agreed back in 1970. Unable to outdo its predecessor despite that album's travails, *Back In The USA* stalled at number 191 on the *Billboard* 200 chart. This said, as a document that would survive the ravages of posterity and come out fighting the other side, it was a good day at the office for MC5.

The cover photo bears little witness to Landau's brief side hustle as the band's life coach. Playing to every presumption of MC5 as drug-sodden delinquents, the group are caught by Stephen Paley partying backstage at the Grande after a September 1969 show, drenched in ... what? Water? Beer? Rocket Reducer? The dressing-room background seen in similar pics is airbrushed out, leaving the impression of five cheerfully stoned street hustlers trying to sell you back the TV they boosted last week. With the album's title emblazoned above the monochrome image, J. L. Hudson's morality police must have been on double time.

'Tutti-Frutti' 1.28 (Dorothy LaBostrie, Joe Lubin, Richard Penniman)
Little Richard Penniman composed 'Tutti-Frutti' in 1955 while working as a bus station janitor. Specialty Records' boss Art Rupe employed the *nom de musique* Joe Lubin in order to claim undue royalties. Dorothy LaBostrie insisted she, not Penniman, had written the song, inspired by her local drugstore's Neapolitan ice cream. 'A whomp baba loo bop, a whomp bop bop' was how Richard vocalised an imagined drum pattern. The lyrics are about anal sex.

Any or all of these may be valid, but whatever the facts, 'Tutti-Frutti' is as primal as rock 'n' roll gets. And as lewd, given the famous refrain 'Tutti-Frutti, aw rooty' was 'Tutti-Frutti, good booty' politely edited and the chorus was originally worded 'If it's tight, it's all right/And if it's greasy, it makes it easy'. Make of all this what you will, but MC5 stick stolidly to the version that Penniman turned into formative 1950s rock 'n' roll. In 2007, *MOJO* placed 'Tutti-Frutti' first in a survey, 'The Top 100 Records That Changed The World'. A staple of every hard rock band's archetypally set-closing roots medley, the song's 300-odd covers range from the anodyne (Pat Boone) to the raunchy-but-acceptable (Elvis, Richard's own). MC5 opt for the latter, Wayne Kramer's solo leaning towards the rock 'n' roll perfection he and Landau sought. The flimsy production denotes some authenticity, underlined by Danny Jordan's percussive piano. The Georgia Peach would have approved.

'Tonight' 2.26 (MC5)
With the US Army baying for ever more Vietnam blood, Rob sets out several persuasive reasons for taking a pass. Anxious to escape the classroom and the draft, he's unable to hear what his teachers say, unwilling to comply with the military's requests. He's intent only on keeping his raging hormones in check by muscling himself up some nighttime action, leaving tomorrow to take care of itself. Cars, girls, music and sticking it to The Man, then, all pressed via Fred Smith's lyrics – his first for MC5 – into a righteous teen anthem that ticks every box on the rock 'n' roll checklist. In the middle, Wayne and Sonic solo liquidly together, while Dennis gleefully ignores Landau's 'no fills' ruling with a ferocious, Bonnie-&-Clyde broadside from the Thompson gun snare every few bars.

Ahead of the album in 1969, Atlantic put out 'Tonight' as a single, backed by 'Looking At You'. It was one of the best couplings in history. If Wexler's people had put some welly behind the marketing, it could have been among the biggest. *Billboard* was unmoved.

'Teenage Lust' 2.34 (MC5)

In this autobiographical tour of interior adolescent angst, Tyner recalls his Lincoln Park teens and how 'the bitches' drove him nuts. He moves to the city, reasoning that brassy chicks from Metro Detroit are more likely to put out than the shy wallflowers from the 'burbs. When this fails, he hits on the perfect way to relieve his pent-up teenage lust: join a rock 'n' roll band! Who knew? Frustrated nebbish hunter becomes hard-to-get hunted, plump Pontiac accounts clerk morphs into feline sex god and, for every doll on the block, resistance is suddenly futile:

> From now on there'll be no compromising
> Rock 'n' roll music is the best advertising
> Baby I can help, you know I got the guts
> I'll be the healthy outlet for your teenage lust.

Sexist anachronisms notwithstanding, 'Teenage Lust' is merely going where every rock 'n' roll song has ventured since 'Rocket 88', with honesty rather than innuendo. In the hands of MC5, the expression of youthful sexual torment and the cathartic release from enforced abstention is safe, especially when preserved in three perfect chords and another flawless solo from Kramer.

'Let Me Try' 4.14 (MC5)

The album's low point is also its longest. 'Let Me Try' is a laboured attempt at a torch song: a fairly doomed exercise for MC5 at this point in the saga. Tyner advises his partner he'll be the singer to her song – even in 1970, this was a clichéd lyrical trope – and that he will heal the compounded neglect and abuse by helpfully supplying 'pleasure deep inside of you'. The hackneyed words speak to MC5's familiar sexism, although Rob's dastardly plans are clad in concern for the lady's wellbeing, and there's no reason to doubt his sincerity. But if trying a little tenderness is what it'll take to get her into the sack, all good. The maudlin arrangement is seventy per cent the Robert Johnson-via-the-Stones blues ballad 'Love In Vain', and fifteen per cent each Ketty Lester's 'Love Letters' and Lorraine Ellison's 'Stay With Me Baby', without a scintilla of any of those tunes' quality or uplift. MC5 should have written this in 1965; they could have gifted it to P. J. Proby and cleaned up on the royalties.

'Looking At You' 3.01 (MC5)

MC5 follow their dullest tune with one of their greatest. Rob espies a young woman and, entranced by her long hair, is struck by a revelation. As if anything more would ruin the moment, he wants nothing other than to look, and maybe dream – an adolescent dilemma that easily chimes with the teen issues that are all over *Back In The USA*. In his sleevenote to the *Motorcity Rebels* compilation, Mike Davis recalled how the sight of an attractive female enabled Rob Tyner to overcome stage fright: '[It] helped him crawl out from under his rock and express himself like a man,' Mike wrote, a tellingly off-guard, alpha meditation that, even now, speaks to a conformity that's usually veneered with typical MC5 mockery.

In 1968, the original 'Looking At You' was MC5's second single: a pivotal example of what can happen when five stoner dudes and a slaphappy free-jazz freak rent a five-hundred-dollar studio to make some rock 'n' roll. By 1970, even Jon Landau's steamcleaning has not cauterised the song's attack, despite the doubts of some who have journeyed this far with MC5. From Machine Gun's explosive snare intro on, the production's relative light and space allows the breakthrough of those guitar nuances Wayne downloaded from Beck and Townshend. His perfectly resolved use of feedback as he colours Rob's vocal from 1.15 is subtle and quite thrilling, a trick he repeats at the back of a beautifully elliptical solo at 2.01.

Mike described the A-Square original as 'a seven-minute song poem' that became 'a two-and-a-half minute speedball about desire.' Barely two years later, despite the concerns of the bassist and others, MC5's escalating maturity has not diluted that heady brew's power.

'High School' 2.41 (MC5)

To teachers, parents and the folk who spend their leisure hours at the local Elks' Lodge: better let the next generation have their say, or accept the consequences. Tyner issues a veiled threat, one that might even be construed as – gasp – political:

> The kids know what the deal is/They're getting farther out everyday
> We're gonna be takin' over/You better get out of the way.

What 'takin' over' meant for these proto-seditionaries was questionable. At this writer's high school – an institution admittedly nearly four thousand miles from Lincoln Park – pupil power went no further than the art class's token hairy clambering onto an upturned milk crate and spouting improvised Marx before a handful of indifferent sixth-formers. Rob may have imagined Mom and Pop grounding the youngsters and thereby triggering society-wide disobedience, but the 5's singer was cannier than that. It doesn't matter: as it motors brightly along on one of the basslines Landau assured the world Mike Davis never played, 'High School' once again strengthens rock 'n' roll's umbilical bond with teen rebellion. Landau claimed the song's lyrics were ludicrous and naïve, according to Mike's *Motorcity Rebels* sleevenote: 'I thought he was supposed to be on our side!'.

'Call Me Animal' 2.05 (MC5)

It's going some when you can write 'Pleistocene' into a song and you're not the Incredible String Band. Short of explicitly recounting one or other sexual conquest (see 'Kick Out The Jams', 'Come Together' *et al*), 'Call Me Animal' is probably the most unusual expression of machismo in MC5's inventory. Far from taking offence that anyone should liken him to a lesser species, Tyner flexes his biceps and revels in his power. The lyric recalls the segue/collision of the man-apes with the gently waltzing space stations at the start of *2001*; or even Jimi Hendrix 'Stand[ing] up next to a mountain' from 'Voodoo Child (Slight Return)': sci-fi machismo, a Nietzschean superman striding tall among the *untermenschen*:

I take a laser beam/And I use it like a stone axe, baby
I take the present, past and future mama
And blast it out my thorax, hey, hey.

Musically, the beauty of the song is in its brevity. 'Call Me Animal' is a superb example of how MC5 have learned, with or without Landau, to dial back their less accommodating tendencies. It's clipped and ringing, with terrific drumming and a dramatic middle break at 1.15.

'The American Ruse' 2.30 (MC5)

At last, ladies and gentlemen, a proper bit of politics, and Tyner's rebuke to a society that routinely lies to and dehumanises its own. Rob must have written the song at around the same time Spiro Agnew, Richard Nixon's vice-president, fingered MC5 from the lineup as part of a heinous North Vietnamese plot to corrupt American youth with drugs and sexual promiscuity. In fact, the clock was running down on both politicians. Agnew, integrity as occluded as his boss's, resigned in 1973 in a murk of criminal conspiracy, extortion, bribery and tax evasion raps. A landslide election result, founded on a vague pledge to achieve 'peace with honor' in Vietnam, would carry Tricky Dicky back to the White House in 1972; but the Watergate Plumbers had taken instruction, and the scandal that would bring down an administration was in play.

Now Tyner lets rip at how freedom, that great constitutional banality, is trumpeted from high school on, despite the omission of an important qualification: that the liberty championed by the Framers has been perverted two hundred years later, and accorded only to those prepared to obey an increasingly conservative and authoritarian line. Overstep the mark, in Tyner's words, and you're beaten 'bloody down at the station' – a predicament to which Rob and the rest of the band could painfully attest. The singer slams America as being 'in terminal stasis, [the air] so thick it's like drowning in molasses', and laments how he's 'sick and tired of paying these dues, and sick to [his] guts of the American ruse'. At 1.18, he enjoins Smith to 'rock 'em back,

Sonic', and the guitarist launches a crisp, Berryesque solo. Fred's suitably skewed few intro bars of 'Battle Hymn Of The Republic' are perfectly judged.

'Shakin' Street' 2.20 (MC5)
Fred Smith's second song on the album bodes well for Sonic's weightier contributions to the third LP, *High Time*. While obeying all the conventions – girls, dudes, kicking out the constrictions of parents and teachers, all in less than 150 seconds of hand-crafted, workingman's ur-punk – Fred sets up a loose narrative around a colourful bunch of homies: Little Orphan Annie, Sweet Sue, Streetlight Sammy, Skinny Leg Pete, Sally Baker and Bobby C. They're part-Bruce Springsteen, part-Lou Reed ('Walk On The Wild Side' minus the junkie transitioning) and part-Damon Runyon, as if the great writer has relocated his bootleggers and bawds from the Big Apple and Broadway to the Motor City and Eight Mile. The identities of those who inspired this crew probably departed with Fred, but they get on down in the titular thoroughfare as to the manner born. Another first for the 5's second guitarist is Smith's duties as lead vocalist, delivering the storyline with a disinterested sneer that seems to match Fred's stoned, deceptively vacant demeanour – something the guitarist would later shake after he married Patti Smith.

The compilation *Motorcity Rebels* features a mainly acoustic rendering of 'Shakin' Street', also produced by Landau, on which Mike Davis asserts he played the Guild D12 twelve-string he acquired with part of Atlantic's signing bonus. 'I was always proud of having supplied the guitar for that track,' he wrote; remembering, of course, Landau's affirmation that Mike had played no part in *Back In The USA*. 'I also got to sing the backgrounds with Fred.'

'The Human Being Lawnmower' 2.23 (MC5)
That MC5 should use oblique metaphor to take potshots at the unacceptable is admirable. It's also possible that Rob's lyrics to 'The Human Being Lawnmower' bewildered many who were criticising MC5 for failing to deliver *Kick Out The Jams* 2.0. In fact, Tyner's loose, Dylanish/poetic excoriation of Vietnam – Rob also came up with the riff and basic musical framework – demonstrates how far he and the 5 have travelled since stiffened nipples and John Sinclair's dreams of disruption. As Rob confirmed to Ben Edmonds, 'The Human Being Lawnmower' symbolises the horror of the war:

> The song starts out in ancient times with a group of killer apes who, as they become more advanced, create a huge machine that kills people. With all their potential for greatness, this is what they create. Their final accomplishment is creating a machine big enough to destroy the entire world.

It's a weird mashup of *2001*, *Planet Of The Apes* and Arnie's *Terminator* movies. At the same time, it's good that MC5 no longer feel the need for a blunt instrument to make every point. The song fades in ominously on a throbbing, single-note bass, Wayne's slashing guitar drawing blood like Elric's Stormbringer, before Rob's bleak warning of how our doom was ordained pre-history:

Can you hear me? Hope you can/Listen here closely you'll understand
There's an ancient race of killer apes/They used a thigh bone
Millimeter by millimeter, millimeter by millimeter
Six times hot as the sun
Didn't mean to hurt anyone/Didn't mean to hurt anyone.

The complexity of 'The Human Being Lawnmower' leaves the song slightly out of kilter on an album so in thrall to the classic procedural conventions of rock 'n' roll. Kramer's solo in what passes for a middle eight starts with a dissonance that matches the song's sentiments, before settling into a splendid break you feel could easily be extended for several minutes if MC5 took off the gloves. Instead Wayne, any danger of lurking psychedelia batted away by Landau, keeps things relatively brief, Tyner's black lyrical vision returning to cap everything off over Dennis' Schmeisser-like snare.

Landau loved the piece. 'Even though [the song] was totally bizarre,' Wayne told Ben Edmonds, 'Jon could appreciate how it was crafted and wanted to record the most condensed and powerful version possible.'

'Back In The USA' 2.26 (Chuck Berry)
With the album already topped by a rock 'n' roll boilerplate, Landau tinkers with the frequency balance to design a tailender that could be booming from the same tinny fifties transistor radio. The 5 bashing out Chuck Berry's classic hymn to Americana recalls Old Glory draped over the band's Grande backline, ironic Motor City tongues firmly in cheeks. But the 5 are so goddam sincere and unaffected that to respond with anything other than dancing feet and a permanent residency of the Crystal Ballroom would be churlish. MC5 pay 'nuff respect to one of the greatest of all rocker anthems, with not a jot of knowing satire or sneery cynicism in earshot. There could never be a more appropriate finale to this fine, endlessly misunderstood album. If MC5 really were the punk prophets, *Back In The USA* – edited where needed – remains the ten commandments.

High Time (1971)

Personnel:
Rob Tyner: lead vocal, harmonica, percussion
Wayne Kramer: guitar, vocal, piano
Fred 'Sonic' Smith: guitar, vocal, harmonica, organ, percussion
Michael Davis: bass, vocal
Dennis Thompson: drums, percussion, vocal
Additional personnel
Charles Moore: flugelhorn, vocal; Pete Kelly: piano; Larry Horton: trombone;
David Oversteak: tuba; Merlene Driscoll, Joanne Hill, Brenda Knight: vocal;
Butch O'Brien: percussion ('Sister Anne')
Charles Moore: trumpet, horn arrangement; Rick Ferretti: trumpet; Leon
Henderson: tenor sax; Dan Bullock: trombone; Ellis Dee, Dave Heller, Dave
Morgan, Scott Morgan, Bob Seger: percussion ('Skunk')
'Lil' Bobby Wayne Derminer' (Rob Tyner): wizzer ('Future/Now')
Skip 'Van Winkle' Knapé: organ ('Miss X')
Kinki Le Pew: percussion ('Gotta Keep Movin'')
Produced: Geoffrey Haslam, MC5
Engineered: Geoffrey Haslam
Recorded at Artie Fields, Detroit; Lansdowne Studios, London
Released: 6 July 1971
Highest chart position: (US Billboard 200) 191

It's a pity Atlantic Records had given up on us at that point – that album
could have turned it around.
Wayne Kramer

It's July 1970. *Back In The USA* is dividing critics and tanking in the charts.
Fans are nonplussed. Is this the same crew who once marched onto the
Grande stage and rattled the bones of the dead? Michael Davis detects change
in both the band and their audience: 'The reception at live performances was
riddled with insults and heckling,' Mike writes. 'We had sold out, that was
obvious.' As the praise is kept hidden, only to come out years later when it's
much too late, MC5 seem to be in unmanaged decline. The critical elements
are atomising; for the first time in ages, the commune is in peril, the living
arrangements separate. The band vacate Hamburg, democratically dividing
co-owned spoils by drawing names from a hat. *Melody Maker*, at least, rates
Back In The USA highly. As empathetic ears await across the pond, MC5 take
off for England.

Mick Farren, journalist, novelist, poet, musician, provocateur and MC5 fan,
invited the 5 to play Phun City, an outdoor festival he was co-organising near
the south coast town of Worthing. On their arrival, the gig promised little.
MC5, The Pretty Things, The Pink Fairies, Kevin Ayers, Mungo Jerry and other
acts soon learned of a severe shortfall in funding owing to a dispute between

Farren's team and the local authority. Strapped for cash, Mick cordially issued a option: play for nothing, or withdraw. (With some irony, the only refuseniks were the London blues-rock band, Free.) Having effectively flown four thousand miles to deliver a gratuity, MC5 weren't best pleased. They'd always wanted to play England, though, and as Wayne remarked, 'to show 'em how it's done'. The 5 proved to be in imperious mood, their bulldozing headline set roadtesting two songs, 'Miss X' and 'Sister Anne', scheduled for the upcoming third album. Ambiguously displaying a warm regard for *Back In The USA* while damning it with faint praise, Wayne told Caroline Boucher of *Disc & Music Echo*:

> We have four worked out onstage now. We always think it's best to work it out onstage first and see what the response is like. I think our second album is perfect. We're not so interested in making a perfect one this time, though.

Just as well, since the group would be without the arch-perfectionist, Jon Landau. Atlantic's interest in MC5 had dimmed following *Back In The USA*'s relative commercial failure. 'Nobody at Atlantic seemed to give a shit about it,' Kramer told Ben Edmonds. 'The people in Michigan loved the first album. It was more like a memento of an MC5 show. The second one they couldn't relate to. Whereas to Europeans, the first one was a little too rough, while the second was right on the money.'

Mick Farren was a talented and prolific writer, a determined ideologue and a genial Furry Freak Brother to his hyperkinetic kinsmen across the water, Abbie Hoffman and John Sinclair. The WPP leader inspired Mick to establish a UK branch of the White Panthers, and later Farren would work extensively with Kramer. Mick was also founder-singer with The Deviants, an obstreperous gang of pre-punks who did for the English underground what MC5 did for America. Farren was happy to chaparone the 5 as they lingered in London after Phun City, tapping his booking-agent contacts for local gigs. At a Farren-brokered date at the Speakeasy, MC5 again snatched defeat from the jaws of victory when two VIP attendees found the Detroiters too loaded to play coherently. Wayne said of their performance that 'we sank to the occasion'. Any enthusiasm expressed by Mick Jagger and Charlie Watts remains unrecorded.

MC5 recorded *High Time* between autumn 1970 and the following spring, at the desk an Atlantic staffer, Geoffrey Haslam. Likened by Kramer to 'a mild-mannered English professor', the engineer had made his bones with the Velvets and J. Geils and was more amenable to free collective bargaining than the autocratic Landau. As Mike Davis told Brett Callwood: '[Haslam] was giving us the wheel and telling us to steer where we wanted to go.' First in the can was Sonic's 'Sister Anne', which the 5 recorded on Atlantic's dime at Lansdowne Studios, which occupied a Grade II-listed Arts & Crafts conversion in leafy Notting Hill. With the beady eyes of Atlantic's bookkeepers on the clock, the 5 returned to Detroit, and a small downtown studio owned by Artie Fields, a former 1940s bandleader.

Buoyed by the relaxed atmosphere, MC5 completed an album many would consider their best. Songs were no longer attributed to the band, but to named writers: a recognition of the individual, instead of the collective, that could have symbolised MC5's journey from rigid Sinclairite dogma to a less polarised ideological mainstream. Once again, political content was thin, while the credits *volte-face* also revealed the escalating influence of Fred Smith, who wrote four of the eight tracks. Kramer claimed two, while Tyner and Thompson were limited to just one each: a division of labour on which MC5's imminent future might have rested.

Session guests included the Detroit trumpeter Charles Moore, whose horn notation for Fred's 'Skunk' was reproduced by musicians who, according to Wayne, 'were used to playing [in] an avant-garde kind of way.' This was ambrosia to MC5, especially after one studio boffin complained about the hired guns' rowdy interpretations of Moore's charts. Echoing Tera Shirma 1966 and the first 5 single, Kramer channelled his inner Trogg: 'This is *exactly* what we want them to do. We want it to be 'BREEEEEEAAAHH!' Even Davis stepped up. 'His sound was important,' Wayne confirmed. 'We came to terms with the idea that the wild shit that he played sounded good.'

High Time has been compared with the near-contemporary fourth album by The Velvet Underground. Since *Loaded* was also an Atlantic release part-produced by Haslam, the view feels more like lazy convenience than thoughtful analysis. Yet most aficionados agree that the Velvets' second LP since the departure of founding partner John Cale, leader Lou Reed not far behind, was the sound of gears being slammed into reverse. The loss and/or indifference of the Velvets' creative core left *Loaded* a watery, if craftsmanlike shadow of its three inspiringly damaged predecessors. *High Time* is as distant from *Back In The USA* as that album is from the 5's first – indeed, as *Loaded* is from its own forerunners. It's as if MC5 and Haslam are retro-fitting production values from the overdriven heavy rock of *Kick Out The Jams* without the distractions – fussy engineers notwithstanding – of convulsive free jazz, dropped strings and other explorations and all-too-human frailties.

This is no bad aspiration, given the 5's burgeoning maturity. But the new album would feel more commanding if the previous record had been half as insipid as its more vocal detractors insisted. *Back In The USA* had captured the unpeeled spirit of the classic form without descending to the paralysing, good-ol'-rock 'n' roll clichés of tribute acts like Wild Angels and Shakin' Stevens, not to mention numerous bands of higher calling who deflated their onstage epics with the obligatory encore medley of 'Lucille', 'Jailhouse Rock' and 'Roll Over Beethoven'. The much-maligned 'shallowness' of MC5's second album actually allowed the music to live and breathe; for all Landau's sins – and years before the dense, Spectorish, sax-driven textures he weaved with

Bruce Springsteen – he seemed to understand that less is more: a laudable attribute for any record producer, especially one as untried.

By comparison, *High Time* is a busy sonic stew, its layered instrumentation sometimes clogged and impervious, seeking more life-giving oxygen than Haslam has released. Bustling production aside, most tracks on *High Time* are longer than those of the second record, suggesting another disconnect between Landau's Talibanic quest for bareback simplicity and Haslam's Zen tendency to allow the band to have at it. Perhaps it's the benefit of hindsight, of appreciating the trio of LPs afresh six decades after release, but to these unfashionable ears *High Time* sounds the least inspired of the three.

For many, Kramer among them, the album was the high point. In 2018, he explained to Jim Kerr how MC5, having survived the febrile bearpits of live performance, had discovered how creatively to work the more intimate environment of a recording studio. Sadly, it was a lesson learned too late:

[*High Time]* is certainly the best album. Marshall McLuhan talked about 'hot' and 'cool' media. When you go to a gig, you're there, you're in it, that's a hot medium. Listening to records, radio and podcasts, they're cool media; the adventure is cerebral, and it's a different canvas from performing live. We finally learned how to [use the studio] on the third album, and it's my favourite of the three.

In September 1971's *Rolling Stone*, Lenny Kaye nailed the view of many:

It seems almost too perfectly ironic that now, at a time in their career when most people have written them off as either dead or dying, MC5 should power back into action with the first record that comes close to telling the tale of their legendary reputation and attendant charisma. This may appear particularly surprising, given the fact that the group's live performances have been none too cosmic of late, but then the old saw is that you can't keep a good band down, and it's never been more forcefully put than here.

Still, Kaye walked back his enthusiasm, echoing Kramer's admission (see earlier) that MC5 had a habit of top-loading and shooting their bolt too soon:

High Time is [not] a perfect album, by any means. Most of side two, with the exception of a lovely little chorus run in Fred Smith's 'Over And Over', doesn't hang together exceptionally well. A large part of the songs seem incomplete, written around chord progressions that quickly wear thin and words that display the lower edge of the school of right-on lyrics.

In 1992, rock scribe and another long-time 5 fan, Dave Marsh, recalled with sadness how *High Time* signalled the end for MC5. 'Hard drugs had entered the band members' lives, and within a year they'd split up, drifting off into

Above: A youthful MC5, circa 1965, possibly sponsored by the Detroit hairdressers'
union. From left to right: Rob Tyner, Fred Smith, Wayne Kramer, Michael Davis, Dennis
Thompson. (*Alamy*)

Below: What a difference three years and several cases of Rocket Reducer make: MC5
in the famous press shot for *Kick Out The Jams*, 1968. From left to right: Fred, Michael,
Dennis, Wayne, Rob. (*Getty*)

Above: Onstage in 1964, a booted 'n' suited MC5 fight a losing battle with fans and equipment. From left to right: Wayne, early drummer Bob Gaspar, Mike, Rob, Fred (cut off in his prime).

Right: Detroit's newest swingin' popsters, circa 1965. From left to right: Rob, Wayne, Dennis, Mike, Fred. Did their mothers know they were out? (*Emil Bacilla/ Lincoln Park Historical Museum*)

Left: A spangly MC5 taping the first album before the right-on faithful at the Grande Ballroom, 31 October 1968. Note John Sinclair at stage right, loitering hopefully with his saxophone.

Right: Pre-classic MC5 in conference, 1963. From left to right: bassist Pat Burrows, drummer Bob Gaspar, Wayne Kramer, Rob Tyner (working up his Pontiac accountant's look), Fred Smith.

Left: Bassist Mike Davis wrote a fine memoir entitled, colourfully if inaccurately, *I Brought Down The MC5*.

Right: Fred 'Sonic' Smith assumes the position at the Grande.

Left: The chaotic final sleeve design for *Kick Out The Jams* proved disappointing. Elektra's Bill Harvey lurks in the top right, inserted into the layout by the art director, Bill Harvey. (*Elektra*)

Right: MC5 in their Sunday best for the second album. Controversial and much-maligned, *Back In The USA* remains punk's sacred text and a great rock 'n' roll record. (*Atlantic*)

Left: The third album, *High Time*, was MC5's most professional, if lacking its predecessors' frantic inspiration and energy. It boded well, but by 1971, the 5 were running out of road. (*Atlantic*)

Right: Activist, writer, British connection and great friend to MC5, Mick Farren, singing with his band, The Deviants, in London's Hyde Park, 1968. (*Shutterstock*)

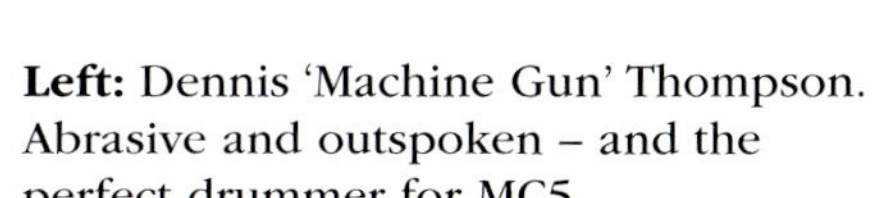

Left: Dennis 'Machine Gun' Thompson. Abrasive and outspoken – and the perfect drummer for MC5.

Right: Wayne wrings the sweat from his Strat, obscuring Sonic throwing similar shapes, 'as if choreographed by Timothy Leary'. (*Getty*)

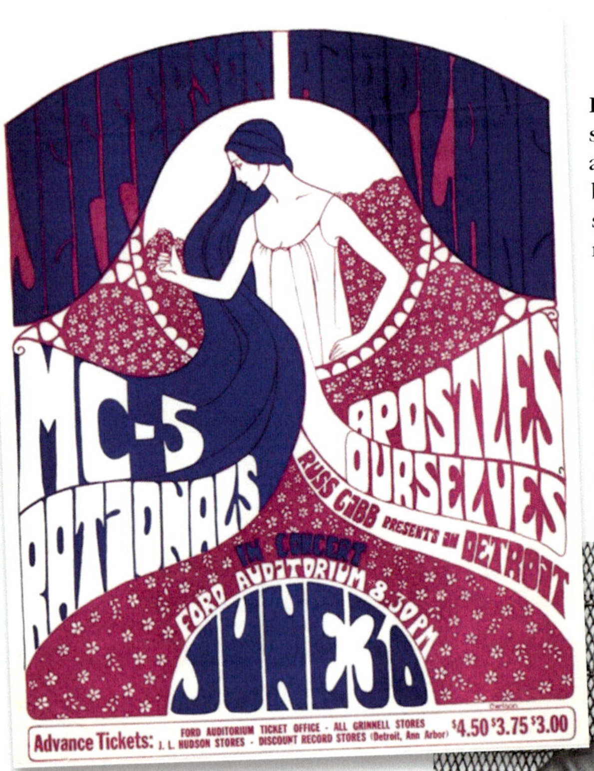

Left: After this 1967 gig supporting Jefferson Airplane at Ford Auditorium, former benefactor Bruce Bennington stopped by with two cops to repossess MC5's equipment.

Below: Though they had real skin in the game, Huey P. Newton's Black Panthers strongly influenced John Sinclair's White Panther Party; the manager saw MC5 as the WPP house band.

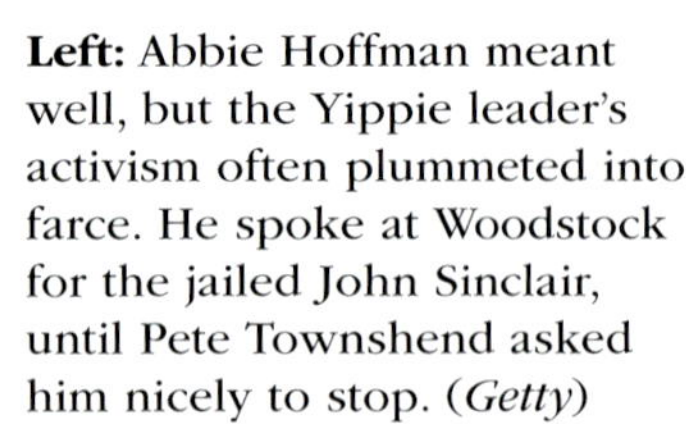

Left: Abbie Hoffman meant well, but the Yippie leader's activism often plummeted into farce. He spoke at Woodstock for the jailed John Sinclair, until Pete Townshend asked him nicely to stop. (*Getty*)

Right: The eccentric Afrofuturist Herman 'Sun Ra' Blount was the world's foremost free-jazz big-band leader and an early MC5 inspiration. Sometimes, he even beamed down from Saturn to share a stage.

Left: The art of the deal with John Sinclair. The Detroit poet, activist, hustler, mover and shaker guided MC5 from 1967 until his imprisonment for possession two years later. (*David Fenton/ Getty*)

Right: Another free-jazz influence, Archie Shepp once likened his sax to a Vietcong fighter's rifle. The great tenorist is seen here at the 2013 London Jazz Festival.

Left: In this Fender promo video from the 2000s, Wayne recalled MC5's visual style and the band's 'total assault on the culture'.

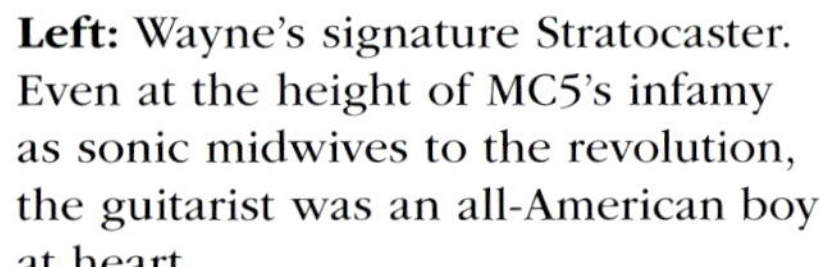

Left: Wayne's signature Stratocaster. Even at the height of MC5's infamy as sonic midwives to the revolution, the guitarist was an all-American boy at heart.

Left: In 2024, *Heavy Lifting* was meant to be a Wayne Kramer solo album until producer Bob Ezrin convinced him otherwise. A decent modern rock album, but MC5 in name only. (*Getty*)

various other configurations,' Marsh wrote in the sleevenote to the CD reissue. 'At least two members wound up in federal prison on drug charges, and they never did reunite before the untimely death of Rob Tyner.'

As *High Time* followed its predecessors to the bargain dumpsters, the beancounters took flight. When, badly broke, MC5 tried to pin down the slippery Dee Anthony, Atlantic's president, Ahmet Ertegun, read them the riot act: 'In the music business we have a concept called not sending good money after bad,' Ertegun intoned, 'and we're not going to do that with you guys anymore.' In 1972, Jerry Wexler moaned to *Rolling Stone*: 'No sales and enormous debt. [MC5] cost us $128,000 we'll never see again.'

High Time's sleeve image is sometimes compared with that of The Rolling Stones' *Let It Bleed*: a homely domestic staple depicted in oddly unsettling disorder. The Stones had Delia Smith's cake balanced on a record-player spindle – okay, with a load of other stuff as well, but stay with me – while the 5 went for a jolly kiddies' alarm clock adorned with the band's faces. Although pre-TV Delia's cherry-popping indulgence made it intact to the Stones' front cover, only to be surrealistic landfill by the time it got round the back, MC5's toytown timepiece looks as if it's been hurled at the wall and photographed where it fell, the hands stuck at five o'clock, little cogs and wheels spread across a red-brown ground. Perhaps it was all a sly tilt at Atlantic's clockwatchers.

'Sister Anne' 7.23 (Fred Smith)

After what too many considered the unbearable lightness of being *Back In The USA*, the power-crazed heavies of *Kick Out The Jams* return. The energy levels on display in Sonic's touching tale of a raunchy nun are undeniably high, the band rattling percussively away from the grid like a funny car at the Dirty D., no easing back on the throttle until an abrupt change of mood six minutes later. At 2.07, Fred and Wayne weigh in with diamond-cutter, Berrylike guitars, followed by duelling blues harmonicas from Tyner and a multitasking Smith. In a first for a band at last permitted to spread their wings, soulful female backing vocals are added courtesy of Freedom Now, a trio of session singers often favoured by Atlantic. Underneath it all another guest, Pete Kelly, bashes away like the barroom pianist who keeps going even though it's 11.30pm and everyone's upending the tables.

Aye, there's the rub. Without wishing to be the spectre at the feast – given that, for once, band, critics and fans largely agree on the merits of *High Time* and of 'Sister Anne' in particular – the track is so darn *busy*. 'Sister Anne' is one dense, blousy, bustling strumpet, as if the producer has thrown her way everything in the studio not nailed down. If Jon Landau's hand rarely strayed from a rigidly oriented tiller, Haslam seems asleep at the wheel, singers and instrumentalists backing blindly into each other as they flounder around in the nourishing but excessively rich gumbo of sound. At 6.05, the song already having outstayed its welcome by a good two minutes,

Charles Moore's horns arrive and whisk MC5 from Notting Hill to New Orleans, there to squeak a mournfully anomalous marching coda that must have taken a wrong turn after leaving the Preservation Hall. To which the only question is 'why?', other than to remind us that this *is* MC5, and there really needn't be a reason.

In a rare instance of MC5 interfacing glancingly with labelmates Yes, bassist Chris Squire – 'a genial cat', according to Kramer – kindly ran home for one of his Rickenbackers after Mike Davis encountered problems with his own instrument. As for the bawdy Bride of Christ herself, 'Sister Anne' may refer to a character from the French folk tale 'Bluebeard', via Shirley Jackson's 1959 gothic horror novel 'The Haunting Of Hill House'. Remembering, of course, the name of MC5's rented Ann Arbor mansion back in 1968. Spooky, or what?

'Baby Won't Ya' 5.32 (Smith)

Fred's bright, upbeat 'Baby Won't Ya' begins promisingly, as Sonic slices his way into a hoarse yelp from Tyner and the band plough into a beefy, stop-start rhythm. The singer embarks on the latest in the unusual narratives that are beginning to inhabit Sonic's songwriting in the wake of 'Shakin' Street' and its lairy crew of ragamuffins. Another five years would lapse before Lenny Kaye introduced Fred to New York's punk poet, Patti Smith, subsequent to which the pair were able to wed without too much inconvenient paperwork. For now, his flair for a lyric suggests kindred spirits had been waiting a minute to find each other.

Patti was, of course, a Dylan nut. And the Bard of Duluth is all over 'Baby Won't Ya', both in the structure of the chorus (reminiscent of 'Baby Let Me Follow You Down'; covered by Bob for his first album, the traditional folk song was bowdlerised by Bert Berns and Wes Farrell as 'Baby Let Me Take You Home' for Brit invasion band The Animals in 1964); and a lively lyric in which the storyteller likens himself to a 'drunken sailor' too long out 'sailin'' on the seven seas' and looking for action – even if it's with the 'strychnine poison woman' he checks out from his window. Peopled by 'tipsy gypsies dancin'' up and down the street', the 'female mercenary coming home from the war' and the witchy Latina who finally relieves his frustrations, Sonic's world is a soft white underbelly of little vignettes and colourful archetypes, a bustling boondocks where the only way for our hero to beat the heat is to get physical – but only in a good way.

Again, 'Baby Won't Ya' is an aural soup prepared with too much seasoning, and the band probably leave the song bubbling for too long. But the crunching refrain and vividly Runyonesque conceits are tasty enough to temper the excess.

'Miss X' 5.08 (Wayne Kramer)

Not even the hallowed portals of Broadway's Brill Building, alma mater of American pop icons from Bacharach & David to Phil Spector, were secure against MC5 and the Detroit Lean. The 5 decide against storming into reception demanding entry by force of arms, and it's probably for the best. Wayne's polished power ballad showcases an unexpected pop sensibility: something the band attempted, but didn't quite manage to draw upon with the previous album's 'Let Me Try'. A ghostly piano intro is enveloped in a subtle reverb, setting up Dennis's heavily compressed drums doing their best not to run aground in the moody undercurrents. Wayne's bluesy guitar curls ominously beneath the words while Rob emotes dramatically, an opera house diva on leapers. Taken at half the pace of almost everything else by MC5, the song has a portentous atmosphere that doesn't really meld with the song's subject. Which is, once more, sex.

Brill habitués such as Neil Sedaka and Lesley Gore were not known to contemplate eroticism this explicit, at least not in front of their agents. Kramer's lyric mines Rob's carnal seam from 'Come Together', a sweatily blow-by-blow account of a strenuous bout of horizontal bopping. Who knows the identity of the titular voluptuary? Calling her 'Miss X' feels overcautious, evasive even, a spy code suggesting the tryst was somehow dishonourable. Perhaps Wayne was setting free his inner gentleman while conveying a sense of intrigue, preserving her dignity (and his own safety, should a cuckolded husband come to call). Perhaps he didn't know her name anyway. If she'd been fifty per cent of a rock 'n' roll road encounter, the tension and sensuality of the song certainly suggests she left her mark, as a figure of seductive, visceral allure.

'Gotta Keep Movin' 3.24 (Dennis Thompson)
'Gotta Keep Movin' marks the drummer's maiden voyage as an MC5 songwriter. It's a terrific debut, closer in spirit to the stripped-back, top-down rock 'n' roll of *Back In The USA* than any other track on *High Time*. There's plenty of wind in the hair and little of the boxed-in weightiness that burdens much of the album. The song rattles along on the writer's piledriven drums and Rob's swinging additional percussion, with Wayne and Fred's cutthroat guitars the fantasy consequence of Chuck Berry scoring meth off Jeff Beck in a Detroit alleyway. In 1998, Dennis told Ken Shimamoto how he wrote 'Gotta Keep Movin' to showcase Sonic's nascent facility to play thirty-second notes and to goad Kramer into an even better performance: 'Wayne said, I'm not gonna let that fucker show me up. So that's exactly what I wanted, was a battle of the two guitar players, and it turned out pretty damn fine.'

Besides playing divide-and-rule with his guitarists, Dennis sticks to MC5's tried and trusted themes of youthful angst, pleading with the usual suspects – teachers, parents, politicians – for the freedom to be what he wants. It's a call to keep moving, physically, emotionally and ideologically, while the writer aims an accusatory finger at The Man as the fount of all society's ills:

Presidents, priests and old ladies too
They'll swear on the Bible what's best for you

> Atom bombs, Vietnam, missiles on the moon
> And they wonder why their kids are shootin' drugs so soon
> Young men fightin' for democracy and sacrificed for mediocrity.

With the 'thick drummer' myth of dumb cliché firmly batted away, the songwriter hands off the responsibility for expressing righteous defiance to his regular singer. Rob rises to the occasion like it was one of his own, spitting out his teammate's cautions as he might on a good night at the Grande. With a muscular, propulsive groove and a crisp sense of economy, Machine Gun's modest rocker is one of the highlights of *High Time*.

'Future/Now' 6.21 (Rob Tyner)

Mike Davis's ominous bass fades in on one of Robert W. Derminer's best songs. Rob employs an apocalyptic tableau to predict dystopia and the consequences of a – metaphorical, arguably – nuclear holocaust. Not only is this a warning that we must adapt or die, but also that the very act of making the requisite adjustments will come at a cost. We face partly Hobson's choice, partly Sophie's; damned if we do, fucked if we don't. But Tyner is ambivalent: he could also be cautioning us not to make assumptions about the incoming storm.

Amid all the doomwatching hang faint glimpses of possibility. The future's even bright, provided we embrace it, warts and all, ignoring the 'Screechin' useless martyrs hangin' naked upon the cross'. It's not a million miles from the glib, billionaire optimism of today's tech bros:

> Forget their logical desperation/Utilise your imagination
> The future's here right now if you're willing to pay the cost.
> The power crazy leaders/Who control your very fate
> They would twist your will/Steal your life, and sell your soul away
> If you're drifting or wandering lost
> You're the perfect target for the double cross
> Freedom's yours right now, if you rule your own destiny.

Throughout the song, Mike's bass grumbles away like a drunken uncle at Christmas, at 1.30 securely mooring a middle break marked by Wayne and Fred in their finest, fighting form. At 3.15, the most surprising moment in the musical history of MC5: in a lingering, three-minute coda, the 5 predict a moody, post-synth Depeche Mode, as sinister electric guitar arpeggios accompany a distant vocal from Rob, a despairing spit for Dave Gahan as he ruminates on the bleak future to which our follies could deliver us, what the planet could look like in the aftermath, and an enigmatic hope for renewal:

> As our mind explodes in a post-atomic dawn
> The future breaks like a tidal wave, engulfing everyone

Confusion and chaos, the trauma of birth
A strange new day for the people of the Earth
Traditions burned away by that rising sun.

'Poison' 3.24 (Kramer)
In a 2018 interview with *Songfacts*, Wayne Kramer told of symbolising the corruption he saw all around him in America and, most immediately, in Detroit:

> These giant manufacturing facilities that forged the steel that went into automobile manufacturing were spewing tons of pollutants into the air ... if you were coming down into Pittsburgh, Detroit, Newark, New Jersey or Gary, Indiana, you would see this line where the air turned brown as you descended down to the airport ... This was really a poison, but the poison was larger, and it was more pervasive than just in the air. It was in the way that big business controlled government.

The outcome was a song for which Wayne had enough regard to re-parcel for post-MC5 gigs and his 1994 solo album, *The Hard Stuff* ('the definitive version,' as the guitarist described his self-produced effort. He wasn't wrong). Although 'Poison' is a decent hard-rock workout, unfortunately Wayne's figurative lyrics are cluttered and unfocused. Taking lead vocal, seemingly he's in several minds about who are the purveyors of society's eponymous toxins and who are the victims. The ambiguities march relentlessly through the song:

The partisans not the artisans are doing their dirty show
But I ripped my pants doing some dance that I learned in France
And they think there ain't nothin' to know
Used, abused, locked up, beaten and fined
But I got free, copped a plea, and I can see
That there ain't no freedom bell gonna chime this time.

At first Kramer appears to favour 'the artisans' (or creators: of art, automobiles or anything else) over 'the partisans' (ideologues and blind-faith believers in political solutions, irrespective of practicality). For a no-bullshit, bluecollar musician this makes sense; Wayne was good people, and a creator, drained by years of soapboxing 'partisan' firebrands bristling with right-on dishonesty. But immediately a perplexing caveat leaves doubt over the guitarist's sympathies. And while the federales had already taken more interest in his personal welfare than he'd liked, the colourful DA-speak 'copped a plea' was still more Kojak than Kramer (until 1974, that is, when the Drug Enforcement Agency offered Wayne, by then virtually a hero of Detroit's criminal underworld, a reduced custodial sentence for heroin distribution in return for shopping his business associates – he refused).

Following a murderous guitar solo which saves the song, Wayne croons a litany of ideological platitudes – 'truth and love are my law and worship, form and conscience my manifestation and guide', etc – condensing the White Panthers' ten-point gospel down to a Utopian wishlist no-one short of the John Birch Society or the KKK could contest. Recited rather than sung over the band's vamping and his own extended soloing, it's all rather melodramatic. No reason to suspect the writer's sincerity, though – even if the partisans finally have the artisans beat.

'Over And Over' 5.13 (Smith)

It's 1971. The youth revolution is in disarray. Abbie Hoffman and four Chicago co-defendants are indicted for intent to incite a riot while crossing state lines. John Sinclair is in prison. Pun Plamondon, already jailed for, er, littering, goes down, pending appeal, for the more street-cred 1968 bombing of an Ann Arbor CIA office (an offence in which the WPP leader is also implicated). Worried the White Panthers could be mistaken for white supremacists, Sinclair changes the movement's name to the Rainbow People's Party. Ahead of a massive reelection majority the following year, Richard Milhaus Nixon, not Pigasus, is POTUS. And still the Pentagon stands, solidly embedded in the DC substrate.

Ever the rock 'n' roll bellwether, Hoffman's *bête noire* Pete Townshend astutely chronicled the prevailing disenchantment in 'Won't Get Fooled Again', a song whose wry affirmation that you just couldn't trust nobody nowadays was echoed by the best song on MC5's valedictory album. The penultimate track on *High Time*, 'Over And Over' probably ought to have been its swansong, the tone archetypally polemical and aggressive compared with that of 'Skunk', the actual finale. From the hesitant reverb of the guitar intro and Dennis's power-driven opening shots, the 5 pile in like the Sparta 300, the tune gaining an irresistable momentum with every stanza and marshalling the unfiltered defiance so long MC5's USP. With the familiar anguished plea to be heard and understood, Fred picks apart the fragmented voices telling him what to think and do, over and over, 'While the cat next door spends all his time trying to think up new anti-social crimes'. He advances no resolution or easy answers, merely evoking an endless cycle of struggle, louder and louder. 'This is the power of The MC5, captured for posterity,' 5 biographer Brett Callwood opined, 'singing about Vietnam, whores, pimps and Uncle Sam.'

On Sonic's lyrical tics, the crime of rhyming 'evolution' or 'revolution' with 'solution' had carried a custodial sentence ever since Bob Dylan taught the world to upend an iambic pentameter. Having already dropped the cinder-block couplet on 'Sister Anne', Fred repeats the offence on 'Over And Over'. Such is the song's power and forward thrust, however, he's off the hook.

'Skunk (Sonically Speaking)' 5.31 (Smith)

With its intro of frenetic drums, whistles and field hollers, 'Skunk' sounds as if Geoff Haslam has ordered up support from Santana's timbales players with a side of Osibisa for good measure. The session pugilists are actually Bob Seger and numerous other hired buddies, all crowding into the studio and bashing hell out of whatever might be seconded for percussion duties. In the middle of it all sits Dennis Thompson, an unstoppable force of nature visiting several flavours of cruelty on his innocent Ludwigs. After 1.10, MC5 muster in full combat readiness, Wayne (or Fred) churning up the rich percussive turf while Fred (or Wayne) slices into the muddily enjoyable racket with sudden, laser-sharp bursts of guitar. At 3.38, following a Kramer solo slightly down in the mix, the much heralded horns turn up, and MC5's last stand becomes the kind of untethered row that would surely have had Jon Landau reaching for the smelling salts.

Despite the Sun Ra connection and the band's love of the avant-garde, mainstream jazz (and jazz-lite confections *pace* Chicago, Ides Of March and BS&T) was another country for MC5. While there are many noble exceptions, some rock bands – think especially The Doors, and producer Paul A. Rothschild's wrongheaded decision to stick a brass section on *The Soft Parade* – have added extracurricular saxes, trumpets and trombones, the outcome middling to unsatisfactory. Luckily the horns on 'Skunk (Sonically Speaking)' are elastic and noisy; not quite as freeform as John Sinclair's once his embouchure was sunk into a Pharaonic solo, but informal enough to belie the fact that Charles Moore's men are reading from charts. They're sufficiently MC5 to hide the join that was so glaringly obvious in Rothschild's work with Morrison and co.

Once again, Rob's vocals sound as if he's been bricked into the wall of sound. Fred allows his singer little in the way of coherent narrative, instead stringing together a vivid collage of punch-drunk sedition and lysergic wit. There are allusions to survival and resistance, nods to radical politics and sly references to Detroit street culture. Above all, the lyrics serve as another instrument; rhythmic, percussive and life-giving, shooting still more concentrated acid into the song's venous system. And in the death, an optimistic hint of better days to come – with or without MC5:

Oh baby, off we go, headin' for a brand new place
The song's been sung, the deed's been done
Staring you right in the face.
Baby, baby, watch your step
You know you really ain't seen nothing yet.

If only that were true.

The End

> Before anyone knew it, the bad, belligerent, and dangerous MC5 were
> reduced to becoming a bunch of damn junkies. It stopped us cold and
> cooked everyone's nuts.
> Dennis Thompson

With *High Time* another commercial flop and Atlantic Records ruefully
comparing notes with fellow corporate malcontents Elektra, an entrepreneur
and MC5 fan, Ronan O'Rahilly, flew the band back to Europe. The Irish
businessman's immediate objective was to win his new charges a contract in
the Netherlands with Philips Records. Naturally the company wanted to check
under the hood, so an outdoor festival appearance was scheduled. In the
honourable tradition of outdoor festivals everywhere, the 5's set was pushed
back till dawn, leaving the band with little else to do for 28 hours than
gobble Mandrax and drink. Eventually they were so blitzed they couldn't play
and Rob Tyner fell off the stage. The Philips execs walked.

Next O'Rahilly, one of Phun City's thwarted backers and the man behind
the offshore pirate broadcaster Radio Caroline, introduced the band to a self-
help programme called 'Ourselves'. By now MC5's refried synapses needed all
the self-help they could get, but the regime – based loosely on concepts
developed by the Boston-born 'spiritual teacher' Ram Dass (aka Richard
Alpert, a former acid buddy of Timothy Leary) – succeeded only in trading
Sinclairite scheming for O'Rahillyite psychobabble. Kramer explained how
MC5's best selves had first to get past their day jobs: 'If we could just get
everyone into [the] Loving Awareness idea, then everyone in the world would
have a beautiful creative existence,' he told Ben Edmonds. 'Unfortunately, it
didn't mesh well with heroin.'

For years, the band had collectively smoked weed, sniffed glue and dropped
LSD. Davis admitted to shooting meth as early as MC5's first single. Now the
native perils of the recording industry, the inability to cope with its less
honourable practitioners and a collective addiction to self-harm were pushing
the 5 ever further into the red. With Mike and Dennis's respective musical
chops already bruisingly interrogated during the recording of *Back In The USA*,
both sought solace in the jazz drug. And while Rob, the eternal beatnik, stuck
to the 'safety' of cigarettes, coffee, beer, reefer and the occasional 'lude, Wayne
and Fred spiralled like their rhythm section into a chasm of smack abuse.

It's December 1971. A rally is held at Ann Arbor's Chrysler Arena before an
audience of 15,000. Demanding the release of John Sinclair are the great and
the good of hip America, among them Bob Seger, Archie Shepp, Stevie
Wonder, Allen Ginsberg and the Ono-Lennons. MC5 are deafening in their
absence; although Kramer has petitioned to play, his calls to the organiser,
Sinclair's brother David, are left unanswered. One day before the concert, the

Michigan Senate approves a bill that will cut the maximum penalty for marijuana possession from ten years to 90 days. By Monday, Governor William Milliken has signed the bill and Sinclair, with time served, is free.

MC5 soldiered on through 1971. Gigs were thinning, the creative chaos the 5 once harnessed fast becoming a liability. Post-Tet, post-JFK, RFK and MLK, post-Manson, post-Altamont, the counterculture had become an opiate-blighted joke. Although MC5 were only ever reluctant fellow travellers on the Sinclair-Hoffman-Motherfuckers oblivion express, the band were still perceived as hitched to the insurrectionists' creaking war wagon, too junked out to jump off. 'Everything seemed so contrived,' Mike said. 'We were still having to talk about 'the revolution' and all this stuff we didn't believe in any more. I started medicating myself to just avoid the whole situation.'

A series of European dates organised by O'Rahilly from February 1972 began ominously when Mike missed the plane. By the bassist's own admission, he was 'swallowing barbiturates like they were jellybeans', earning more money slinging product in Detroit than playing with the band. Arriving in England, his keenness and 'wild shit' fled and everyone agreed he should quit. Putting a frumpy suburban London wrap on the years of cool Motor City craziness, Mike reportedly played a final gig with MC5 at the Greyhound, a pub in Croydon which would become a birthing pool for Britpunk. (As with most of the events of MC5's final months, timelines are vague, their provenance often dependent upon who's recounting the tale. Mike was definitely still around on 11 February 1972, the evidence a YouTube video of the original band at Friars, Aylesbury, delivering a coruscating version of 'Tonight'.)

The 5 dated in Cambridge with Syd Barrett's Stars, and in Canterbury with Marc Bolan's former Tyrannosaurus Rex percussionist, Steve Peregrin Took. Fred Smith contacted a long-term British pen-pal, bassist Steev Moorhouse, who helped the band fulfil some of the European shows. Moorhouse was proficient and the 5 were keen to keep him, but he was committed to his own group. Steev was replaced by Derek Hughes, secured by Kramer through an advertisement in Germany, followed by Ray Craig for US dates only.

Back in Britain, O'Rahilly was making an *Easy Rider*-style movie, *Gold*, for which the Dubliner required a musical score. 'The film was awful, but I didn't care because I liked the challenge of writing music for film,' Wayne explained. 'It was just Fred, Dennis, Rob and me. I played bass on the session, and we came up with some of the most progressive music we'd ever made.' The 5-lite recorded 'Gold', 'Train Music' and 'Inside Out', the latter two songs released on a vinyl soundtrack album which now sells for around £80, if it's around at all. 'Gold', however, can readily be found on the indispensable 2008 MC5 compilation, *Motorcity Rebels* (see below). Created by the band playing to the film in real time, the three tracks hinted at where MC5's instincts, spurred by a couple nights off the dope and a mild dose of adulthood, might have taken them. Their jazz idols were all over these tunes; edgy and loose, the highlights were the guitars and, especially, Thompson's drumming. It was probably still too busy for Jon Landau, but at last Dennis had meshed a sense of discipline into an otherwise typically freeform and frenetic attack.

It seemed MC5 had mileage in the tank. Wayne told *Friendz*'s Nick Kent of plans for another concert album, provisionally entitled *Live On Saturn*; but like much in the 5's universe c1972, the project would remain earthbound. Bootlegs and previously undiscovered deep cuts aside, there'd be no more original MC5 matter until 2024, with the release of Wayne Kramer's final solo shout, *Heavy Lifting* – an MC5 album in name only. In February or March 1972, your servant caught MC5 live at London's Seymour Hall, at which corroded memory banks insist Sun Ra was also in the house. Although the 5 and Ra shared billing more than once, this may be more wishful thinking than accurate recall.

In August, O'Rahilly blagged MC5 a place at Wembley on one of the UK's first big stadium rock events. The London Rock and Roll Show's part-lipsmacking, part-indigestible menu billed MC5 heroes (Chuck Berry, Little Richard, Bo Diddley, Jerry Lee Lewis); avuncular, kiss-curled old-timers (Bill Haley); 1960s Anglo-European copyists (Screamin' Lord Such, Heinz); 1970s glamrock deadbeats (Gary Glitter); and numerous acts, past and present, grimly squeezing the juices from yet another engineered nostalgiafest of 'classic' rock 'n' roll. Icons aside, in this company MC5 were doing 120 in a 30 zone, but still they went down badly with the sea of drape-jacketed zealots flooding the sacred turf. The audience forced the 5 to beat an early retreat under a fusillade of beercans, one of which Tyner ill-advisedly returned, causing even more uproar. Things were hardly helped by O'Rahilly decking MC5 out as glam parodists so arch the rhinestone cowboys of the old Grande looked like bank clerks. Did Ronan really think Wayne's gold facepaint, Rob's glittery, electrostatic Afro and Fred's 'Sonic Smith' Marvel Comics getup would demonstrate MC5's dry humour before a crowd not known for its grasp of irony? These were superannuated teddy-boys thrown off the last bus back to 1957, the same gang who'd hurled sharpened pennies at The Who when the former mods co-headlined with rocker aristo Berry at the Royal Albert Hall three years earlier. If only the 5 had modelled their street rigs of leather and denim: 'We were rocking hard enough,' Kramer wrote, 'but once [the audience] decided we were rough trade from Venus, it was all over.' Perhaps the bigger mystery is why O'Rahilly failed to alert the Detroiters to the London crowd's narrow, fiercely expressed partisanship; that Gary Glitter was booed from the stage even faster than MC5 was scant consolation.

Towards the close of a European tour that autumn, Tyner quit. Assuring the singer of better paydays to come, Kramer unsuccessfully tried to talk him down. Smith's overtures ended in fisticuffs. Thompson, by now heavily medicating and reduced to skimming from the group's already dwindling coffers, retreated back home to detox. Later Rob's wife, Becky, insisted that Dennis had been first to depart MC5 while everyone else was still in Detroit. As well as the management black hole, she pinpointed drugs as the corrosion eating away at the band. In an account that seemed to sum up the substance-infused clowns' workshop now housing MC5 – that, or a particularly lurid episode of *EastEnders* or *All In The Family* – she expounded at length to Edmonds:

> [MC5] went to Europe and hooked up with Ronan O'Rahilly, who later claimed he almost saved the band – and he almost did. But it wasn't enough. Michael had left because of his severe addiction. Dennis was really, really in trouble. Even for Rob, being in the MC5 was becoming difficult. Dennis came over and flat-out said 'I'm not going. There's no money in it, and nothing is working out. It's all horrible.' And Rob said, 'You know what? I'm not going either.' It's always been rumoured that Rob was the first person to quit the band, but it was really Dennis. A few days later, Fred and Sigrid [the first Mrs Smith] came over to convince Rob to go back to the band. But after dinner, Rob said, 'I'm not going.' Fred then stood up and punched him. Then all four of us started fighting. I yelled, 'Sigrid, get Fred the fuck out of my house now!' Then Wayne started threatening us. He was hanging out with a bunch of gangsters on the East Side, and we literally had to move out of our house because we were in fear for our lives.

Wayne's own telling of the downturn of 1972 puts his 'small-time Detroit criminal' career as post-MC5; in 1975, an unhappy cocktail of petty larceny and dope (using *and* dealing) would send the guitarist to prison for four years. But it's not inconceivable that his shaky condition and mindset led him to numerous ill-starred partnerships on the meaner streets of the Motor City before the band's final car crash. For now, Wayne considered replacing Rob with Bob Seger, then Scott Morgan of The Rationals. Neither was available. Wayne and Fred limped on in Europe with Hughes and Ritchie Dharma, an experienced but unrehearsed drummer sourced by O'Rahilly. Once promoters had discovered the original MC5 had turned into MC2 plus strangers, fifteen gigs were lost in Italy alone. As Kramer wrote, dates were cancelled one after the other:

> There were no rehearsals … Singing MC5 songs was almost completely out of the question. Neither Fred nor I had ever attempted to sing these songs, and had no idea how to go about it. We just tried as best we could to play for the contracted amount of time, to ensure we got paid. The performances had almost nothing to do with MC5.

It's New Year's Eve, 1972. Wayne, Rob, Fred, Mike and Dennis reconvene at the Grande Ballroom. This is no joyful reunion, but a contract killing before a half-empty theatre, the industry picking pennies from dead men's eyes. MC5 had once smoked the American rock circuit like Connie Kalitta on the Thunderbird Dragway. Now they're running on a forecourt attendant's apron.

From commanding a nightly fee of nearly ten thousand dollars, the group have agreed to five hundred. Where once 1,400 fans had occupied the room, now there are barely enough to fill a moshpit. None in the band was in contact with any other before the show. No one knows who is playing what. Nerves are frayed, tempos are slipshod, changes are random. The band's live presence and power, once bulletproof, are atrophied and impotent. MC5 are falling apart in public.

Sadly Kramer and Smith look across at each other. Wayne says, 'I can't take it anymore. I have to leave.' Fred nods in understanding as Wayne exits the stage before the end. They are all still in their early twenties.

Bootlegs, Deep Cuts And 'Black To Comm'

Despite the flaws, the live first album exemplified MC5. Yet that set was incomplete, lacking the one song, usually earmarked as set closer, that rivalled 'Kick Out The Jams' for consideration as the band's psalm, signature and national anthem. 'Black To Comm' was a brutal sonic wrecking ball, the most basic riff imaginable deconstructed, if that's possible, by the Kramer-Smith axis of evil and their demon familiars.

It seemed perverse to omit this lengthy audial meltdown. Imagine The Who forgetting to include 'My Generation' on *Live At Leeds*: it meant *Kick Out The Jams* didn't finally stand up as a complete testament, let alone Brother Crawford's MC5 testimonial. Perhaps 'Black To Comm', a Frankenstein's monster unleashed by the band in 1965 and as typically MC5 as ripped-up contracts and drug busts, was just too extreme for Elektra to foist upon its unwary customers. 'Black To Comm' could certainly be a hard listen; perhaps what Jon Landau was referring to when he described MC5's psychedelic payloads as 'man's inhumanity to man'. But then, 'listening' was academic; once MC5 were roaring away on the Grande stage, few in the audience would be nodding out as if Russ Gibb had just put on the new Tonto's Expanding Head Band album. As the 5 rushed headlong into the collapsing last ten or more minutes of 'Black To Comm', the more likely response was barely containable physical frenzy, even for those with fewer solvents in their neural pathways than the band.

Given the deflating effect of *Kick Out The Jams*' eventual finale, Rob Tyner's insistence that the Devil's Night 'Black To Comm' failed to pass muster for the album's closing cut is odd. Fans were deprived of a decisive live MC5 record, one on which the band could capitalise on a magnificent first four tracks by balancing them with more of the same. It made the 5's sad early demise even harder to bear.

Like every rock vintage, MC5 have been corked by low-quality boots, re-hashes and repetition. The bootleg environment has long been the Wild West for fans of 1960s-70s artists, with the same outlaw material, repackaged and often spuriously marketed as 'definitive' or 'never before released', lurking around every rocky outcrop intent on mugging the incautious collector. Since it's difficult, not to mention costly, to sift through every such malfeasance in order that you, reader, do not have to, there follows a rollcall of those MC5 rehashes and compendia worthy of further investigation, alongside one or two that come attached with definite caveats. If I've missed anything important, my apologies.

Power Trip (1994)

'Looking At You' (instrumental)/'I'm Mad Like Eldridge Cleaver'/'Black To Comm'/'The Pledge Song'/'Head Sounds'/'Powertrip'/'I Put A Spell On You'/'Born Under A Bad Sign'/'I Want You'

Numerous renderings of 'Black To Comm' are scattered across the recorded MC5iverse in varying states of undress. Few do it justice. One that does can be found on this 1994 collection, recorded at several venues between 1968 and 1970 and curated by John Sinclair. Engineer Keith Keller helped Sinclair digitally restore the inconsistent source material, while the ex-White Panther leader thoughtfully slipped into the sleeve insert the WPP 'total assault' statement and ten-point manifesto, alongside a more palatable six-page essay on MC5.

Sinclair's assertion that this 'Black To Comm' was 'relatively tame' was naturally unconnected with the absence of his occasional skronking tenor sax stylings. If shorter than usual, the reading is no less fierce. Distilled to just over seven minutes, the extra-concentrated sonic assault is all-consuming, and a fine companion to 'I'm Mad Like Eldridge Cleaver', an improvisation taped at the Grande on 27 October 1968. Though not a regular part of the 5's live set, 'Eldridge Cleaver' (named after the early Black Panther leader) showed how MC5 could take a simple John Lee Hooker riff, 'I'm Bad Like Jesse James' – in effect, the much-loved 'Boogie Chillun' – and dissolve it into eighteen minutes of atonal, avant-rock madness. This time it's taken apart still further by Sinclair's Sheppisms. Essential.

MC5 Motorcity Rebels: The Definitive Story (2008)

DISC ONE: 'Kick Out The Jams' (1968)/'Shakin' Street' (1969)/'The American Ruse' (1969)/'Skunk (Sonically Speaking)' (1970)/'Tutti-Frutti' (1969)/'Poison' (1970)/'Gotta Keep Moving' (1970)/'Tonight' (1969)/'Sister Anne' (1970)/'Future/ Now' (1970)/'Gold' (1971)/'I Can Only Give You Everything' (1966)
DISC TWO: 'One Of The Guys' (1967)/'I Just Don't Know' (1966)/'Looking At You' (original A-Square single 1968)/'Black To Comm' (1965)/'I Don't Mind' (1965)/'High School' (instrumental 1970)/'Come Together' (1968)/'Baby Please Don't Go' (1966)/'I'm A Man' (1966)/'Look What You've Done Done' (1966)/'Rocket Reducer No.62' (1968)/'Ramblin' Rose' (1970)/Bonus track: 'Sister Anne' (live with Lemmy 2003)
Excellent MC5 collection, notable for a primitive 1965 'Black To Comm', both sides of the first 5 single, the original A-Square version of 'Looking At You' and the fruits of several fine concerts between 1968 and 1970. Some of *Motorcity Rebels* is available elsewhere, but wise collating, beautiful packaging and the entertaining, per-track disquisitions of Mike Davis and Dennis Thompson should sway anyone uncertain of purchase.

The American Ruse (1994)

'Tonight' (instrumental)/'The Human Being Lawnmower'/'Looking At You' (instrumental)/'Looking At You'/'The American Ruse'/'The American Ruse' (instrumental)/'Call Me Animal' (instrumental)/'Tonight'/'Tutti-Frutti'/'Teenage Lust' (instrumental)/'High School' (instrumental)/'Back In The USA'/'I Believe To My Soul'/'Black To Comm'
A Sinclair-compiled pot-pourri of outtakes and works-in-progress that would eventually be disinfected for absorption into *Back In The USA*. Made, as John

trills on the sleeve, 'before the producer had completely stripped the band of its power!', *The American Ruse* is a scattergun prisoner of its reference-track background, lacking in the sense of self that might today make the album a suitably hefty proxy for the 5's second album (which, as we know, Sinclair hated). The demos and instrumentals here evince more beef than some of *Back In The USA*'s final cuts – hints of what might have been are tantalising – but, thrown together without context, they exist in an indeterminate limbo, of interest mainly to MC5 scholars. Who should take special note: Sinclair states in his sleevenote that 'Black To Comm' is the same as the version included in *Power Trip*; ie: recorded at Detroit's First Unitarian Church, 8 September 1968. Far from it; while the latter is arguably the most powerful and cohesive 'Black To Comm' to have made it to release, here on *The American Ruse* it's five minutes longer and terrifyingly freeform, as if the 5 have shipped in Menard's entire stock of Rocket Reducer and are already trading the empties. Perhaps it's similar to what Tyner would deem substandard at the Grande a few weeks later.

Purity Accuracy (2004)

DISC ONE Rehearsals: 'Skunk (Sonically Speaking)'/'Poison'/'Gotta Keep Movin''/'Baby Won't Ya' (Fred Smith guide vocals)/'Sister Anne'/'Future/ Now'/'Over And Over' (acoustic)/'Gold'/'The Pledge'/'Powertrip'/'Tutti-Frutti'/'Tonight'/'Teenage Lust' (instrumental)/'Looking At You' (2nd version)/'High School' (instrumental)/'Call Me Animal' (instrumental)/'The American Ruse'/'Shakin' Street' (acoustic version)/'The Human Being Lawnmower'/'Back In The USA'/'Looking At You' (instrumental)/What is Zenta?
DISC 2 1965-1968: 'Looking At You'/'Borderline'/'Looking At You' (instrumental)/'I Can Only Give You Everything'/'I Just Don't Know'/'One Of The Guys'/'Little Red Riding Grmph'/'I Don't Mind'/'Look What You've Done'/'Baby Please Don't Go'/'Break time'/'I'm A Man'/'Looking At You'/'Black To Comm'/'I Put A Spell On You'/'Born Under A Bad Sign'/'I Want You'/'I Believe To My Soul'
DISC 3 Live at the Saginaw Civic Centre, 1 January 1970: Intro/'Ramblin' Rose'/'The Human Being Lawnmower'/'Tonight'/'Rocket Reducer No.62'/'It's A Man's World'/'Teenage Lust'/'Looking At You'/'Fire Of Love'/'Shakin' Street'/'Starship'/'Kick Out The Jams'/'Black To Comm'/'Teenage Lust'
DISC 4 Live at the Grande Ballroom, 1968: Brother J. C./'Motor City Is Burning'/'I Believe To My Soul'/'Rocket Reducer No.62'/'I'm Mad Like Eldridge Cleaver'/'Ice Pick Slim'/'Black To Comm'
DISC 5 Live at the Sturgis Armoury, 27 June 1968: 'Kick Out The Jams'/'Come Together'/'Revolutionary Blues'/'Rocket Reducer No.62'/James Brown medley: 'Cold Sweat'/'I Can't Stand Myself'/'There Was A Time'/'Upper Egypt'/'Tutti-Frutti'/'Borderline'/'Born Under A Bad Sign'/'I Want You'/'Starship'/'Black To Comm'
DISC 6 Live at the 100 Club London, 13 March 2003: 'Sister Anne'/'Gotta Keep Moving'/'Looking At You'/'Skunk (Sonically Speaking)'

Monstrous – and monstrously expensive – six-disc set of live material, studio demos, deep cuts and early hothousing in Wayne's mum's basement. Most of this stuff is available elsewhere as single volumes – there's a one-disc digest of *Purity Accuracy* trading under the same name – although some may value the extensive content pulled into one big, bouncy box set. However, others might be deterred by the price tag; at time of writing Amazon are offering the full monty for a post-revolutionary £310. With some of the material great, some decidedly ropey, this is for the MC5 completist with patience, the occasional tin ear and plenty of shelf space on the yacht.

Starship: Live At The Sturgis Armory, June 27 1968 (1998)

'Kick Out The Jams'/'Come Together'/'Revolutionary Blues'/'Rocket Reducer No.62'/James Brown medley: 'Cold Sweat'/'I Can't Stand Myself'/'There Was A Time'/'Upper Egypt'/'Tutti-Frutti'/'Borderline'/'Born Under A Bad Sign'/'I Want You'/'Starship'/'Black To Comm'

John Sinclair and Keith Keller were clearly busy during the early 1990s cleaning up MC5 tapes for the public gaze. Their efforts were not in vain. *Sturgis Armory* is superb, not far off *Kick Out The Jams* as an example of MC5 at their primal best. Originally taped on a reel-to-reel through the band's soundboard, its content is identical to Disc 5 of the *Purity Accuracy* collectathon. An earlier CD from 1994, ascribed the rubric *Black To Comm*, comprised the same concert, with the addition of 'Ramblin' Rose' and 'I Believe To My Soul'. Neither was deemed good enough for the later release, while the rest of the recording clearly benefited from the studio diligence of Sinclair and Keller. Notwithstanding MC5's love and respect for the Funkfather, the James Brown medley feels like filler or interlude. Pharoah Sanders' 'Upper Egypt', like 'Starship, is MC5's distantly loose – some would say wayward – reading of the work of a free-jazz icon, with words by John Sinclair. Decent as these interpretations are, it's a relief to get back to familiarity, which was MC5 demonstrating the sensitivies of a panzer division with a savage 'Black To Comm', the famous riff quickly degenerating into a relentless ten-minute maelstrom of white-hot feedback and arrhythmic cacophony. Or, as Sinclair gravely posited in his sleevenote, 'a registration of the band's deepest inchoate feelings of rage and rebellion.' Yeah, right. It was still more about sex than sedition.

Babes In Arms (1990)

'Shaking Street'/'The American Ruse'/'Skunk'/'Tutti-Frutti'/'Poison'/'Gotta Keep Moving'/'Tonight'/'Kick Out The Jams'/'Sister Ann'/'Future/Now'/'Gold'/'I Can Only Give You Everything'/'One Of The Guys'/'I Just Don't Know'/'Looking At You'

Compiled by Wayne Kramer from his private archive, *Babes In Arms* has frequently been repackaged since its first release in 1983 on the fabled New York cassette-only label ROIR. The set comprises outtakes and demos – there's that fascinating, mainly acoustic rendering of Sonic's 'Shakin' Street', offering the worrying intelligence that MC5 sometimes allowed melody to squint out from the white noise – along with the first uncensored version of 'Kick Out The Jams' and the early 45s. The needle-drop recordings of 'One Of The Guys' and 'I Can Only Give You Everything' helpfully retain the original vinyl's pops and crackles. When the maiden A-side was reissued in 1969 by the spurned AMG label, its coupling was 'I Just Don't Know', a Pretty Things-style studio rumpus left over from 1966. With the most interesting tracks now available on the more comprehensive *Motorcity Rebels*, this is no longer the required purchase it once was.

Live Detroit (1988)

Intro/'Come Together'/'I Want You'/'I Believe To My Soul'/'Come On Down'/ 'High Rise'/'It's A Man's Man's Man's World'/'Looking At You'/'Fire Of Love' Culled from gigs at Unitarian Church (8 September 1968) and Westfield High School (10 January 1969), one or two of these performances are pretty good. Unfortunately, you have to get past the cheap cassette recording that renders some of the 5's most famous songs unlistenable (respectfully, I refer m'learned friends to the qualification earlier concerning appropriate response to MC5's live music). 'Black To Comm', for some reason here entitled 'Come On Down' – presumably by a junior compiler at the French record label Revenge, if not a young Drew Carey or Leslie Crowther – is the same twelve-minute racket included on *The American Ruse*. Avoid.

Thunder Express (1999)

'Kick Out The Jams'/'Empty Heart'/'Ramblin' Rose'/'Thunder Express'/'Rama Lama Fa Fa F'/'Motor City Is Burning'/'I Can Only Give You Everything'/'I Just Don't Know'/'Looking At You'/'Borderline' Although definite feelings of déjà vu are provoked by the presence of the first two singles, and Sinclair's ubiquitous Panthers' doggerel in the sleeve note, the first six tracks on *Thunder Express* are worth the admission fee. Lifted from a French TV show taped at Studio Herouville in March 1972, with Steev Moorhouse on bass, the band are full of vim and vigour and tight as a Michigan understeer. Especially noteworthy are a Rolling Stones cover, 'Empty Heart', and a blistering, ten-minute 'Rama Lama', complete with a heavily percussive mid-section.

  Dennis Thompson has rarely been better recorded, inviting comparisons with how good Charlie Watts sounded under the producer of the Stones' *Let It Bleed* and *Beggars Banquet*, the matchless Jimmy Miller – himself a drummer. A dizzying, amyl nitrate must-have.

Motor City Is Burning (1999)

'Kick Out The Jams'/'Come Together'/'Revolutionary Blues'/'The Human Being Lawnmower'/'Tonight'/'Teenage Lust'/'Looking At You'/'Shakin' Street'/'Ramblin' Rose'/'Tutti-Frutti'/'Borderline'/'Born Under A Bad Sign'/'I Want You'/'Starship'/'I Believe To My Soul'/'Black To Comm'

Once again, rough recordings mask what are often excellent performances. Most of these tracks are available elsewhere. The Sturgis Armoury version of 'Black To Comm' gets yet another airing, while ten of the sixteen tracks pop up on another 5 compilation, BMG's *Extended Versions*.

Where Next?

Having been in MC5 has not left any of us independently wealthy. MC5 never pulled a golden horseshoe out of our rear end. We never had the big hit record, which I think is one of the things that endears us to people who are fans of anti-heroes.
Wayne Kramer, interview with Jim Kerr, *Q104.3*, 2018

Rob Tyner

Some years after the fall, Rob worked with a band styled The New MC5, before his disgruntled former colleagues forced him to revert to The Rob Tyner Band, itself evolving into Rob Tyner & The National Rock Group. Following a hookup with Eddie & The Hot Rods (realising a 1977 UK single, 'Till The Night Is Gone'), Rob concentrated on production, helming a 7-inch for (and sometimes singing MC5 covers with) a Detroit group called Vertical Pillows. In 1985, Rob worked with Drew Abbott on *Ambush*, a benefit album for Vietnam veterans clunkily attributed to 'Stev Manteiv', and helped to set up the Community Concert Series with Detroit's Episcopalian Church of St. Andrews. Always a formidable thinker, able to argue the most dubious revolutionary theory with elegance, wit and worldly scepticism, Rob was taken tragically early after a heart attack on 17 September 1991. He was 46.

Fred Smith

In 1973, Fred dragooned Dennis Thompson, Michael Davis (playing piano) and bassist John Hefty into a venture called Ascension (invited to join, Rob and Wayne declined). Although Sonic insisted the name symbolised both band and music soaring to new heights, everything fell after less than a year, a few gigs and one live recording that never made the edit suite. A rough-as-boots live performance survives on YouTube; taped in Detroit, 20 September 1973, it's worth checking out. Better came in 1974 when, with fellow Detroiters Scott Morgan (ex-Rationals), Gary Rasmussen (The Up) and Scott Asheton (The Stooges), Fred formed the short-lived but remarkable Sonic's Rendezvous Band. Live material has since been released, while SRB's sole single of the time, the pyromaniacal 'City Slang', has rightly become a punk classic. Cleverer and more alert than his dead-eyed deportment in MC5 band photos suggested, Fred left Sigrid in 1977 and married the poetic doyenne of Big Apple punk intelligentsia, Patti Smith, in 1980. Just 46, Fred died from heart failure on 4 November 1994.

Michael Davis

Following Ascension, Mike was found guilty of upholding MC5's fine tradition of selling drugs to undercover narcotics officers, residing between 1975 and 1976 at Lexington Federal Prison. There he unexpectedly discovered that Wayne Kramer was a fellow inmate. After a sympathetic judge spotted Mike's prison artworks and awarded early release, the bassist was invited by Ron Asheton to join Destroy All Monsters, or 'the most dysfunctional group ever to set foot on a stage,' as Davis memorialised the influential Detroit noisemongers. On leaving DAM in 1984, he became a silkscreen printer, before moving to Tucson, Arizona, there to toggle autoshop work with brief bass duties to a local band, Naked Prey.

In 1991, MC5's remaining foursome gathered at Detroit's State Theater to play a benefit concert for the Tyner family. Once the hugs and handshakes were done, everything rapidly went south. Clocking on for rehearsal three and a half hours late, Sonic quaffed two bottles of wine and refused to participate for another hour. Mike recorded in his autobiography:

> We slogged it out, with the results being far from anything close to acceptable. We even got into a brief argument about how long the breaks between Rob's vocals were on the verse of 'Kick Out The Jams'. Without Rob to set us straight, there was no resolution. I was making a point to Fred about it, since I was going to sing the song, when he shouted at me at the top of his voice, 'I don't care!'

Although Mike raised the idea of a permanent 5 reunion, Wayne – perhaps bruised by the tantrums of his co-guitarist – questioned whether the band were still commercially viable. Kramer's gloom was reinforced at the concert proper, when Smith's tardiness and disinterest turned a celebration of a friend and a rock 'n' roll life into a humiliating charade. At one point, perhaps the most comically ironic moment of MC5's strange career, someone in the audience shouted 'kick out the jams, motherfuckers!' It may have been a request for the song. Then again, it may not.

By the noughties, as Kramer warmed to the idea of an MC5 renewal, Davis heeded the call and headed for London. The bassist also worked with fellow volunteer musicians to raise awareness of music education in aiding cognitive ability. Bearing the marks of his addictions until liver failure took him at 68 on 17 February 2012, Mike left behind a fine canon of musical and visual art. He also wrote a wry, thoughtful memoir entitled, colourfully if not entirely accurately, *I Brought Down The MC5*.

Dennis Thompson

Dennis followed his gig with Ascension by stints with Sirius Trixon, The Motor City Bad Boys and Dodge Main. He briefly teamed with Ron Asheton in LA's ill-fated New Order (no relation), who self-destructed after singer Dave Gilbert, wasted on angel dust, forgot his lyrics and dried onstage. Dennis then joined New Race, alongside three members of the Australian punk group Radio Birdman. Latterly, he contributed to the partial reunion, DKT/MC5, with Kramer and Davis.

In a 2017 interview with *Spin* magazine, Wayne observed how the work of some of the world's best musicians fed into that of his punchy ex-compadre and, by association, MC5: '[Dennis] listened to Sun Ra and Elvin Jones, Charlie Watts, Keith Moon and Mitch Mitchell. He was able to put these things together in a way that no one else had done before.' If his post-5 career was bitty, Dennis, who died aged 75 on 9 May 2024 following a coronary, remained an astute and typically acerbic commentator, his entertaining observations of the madness and significance of MC5 peppering TV interviews, retrospective magazine articles and reissue CD booklets.

Wayne Kramer

For long after his side trip as accredited partner to the dope fiends of Detroit, Wayne continued to champion MC5, his baby since 1963. In 1975, his experiment in 'illegitimate capitalism' saw him banged up for four years, serving two. On emerging, he cleaned up and got busy, moving to Manhattan and forming Gang War with ex-New York Doll Johnny Thunders. After returning to Detroit to work with Don and David Was's funk experimentalists Was (Not Was), he relocated to Florida and became a carpenter. In 1994, he moved to Los Angeles and, signed to Epitaph Records, began crafting the first of several solo albums, later enlisting the help of soul brother Mick Farren. (Wayne retained an affection for the UK that was warmly reciprocated, remembering who had picked up *Back In The USA* where America had failed, and still venerated the 5's second album as a source text for punk.) Reunited with John Sinclair in 1998, Wayne co-wrote and produced the album *Full Circle* for his ex-manager's band, Blues Scholars. In 2001, assisted by a government small-business loan, he started a boutique record label, Muscle Tone, with his second wife, Margaret Saadi Kramer.

A year later, a feature-length documentary, *MC5: A True Testimonial*, was well received and promised much, playing at film festivals around the world. Eventually hobbled by a dispute over music royalties, the film remains officially unavailable on DVD at time of writing, although 'promo' editions of varying quality can be found online. In 2003, a one-off gig with Thompson and Davis at London's 100 Club – Kramer refused to call it a reunion – was fleshed out by famous English fanboys Lemmy Kilmister (Motörhead), Dave Vanian (The Damned) and Ian Astbury (The Cult). Rapturously received – by now the scales were magically tumbling from the eyes of *arrivistes* and closet MC5 devotees too long in denial – the date was captured on a DVD, *Sonic Revolution: A Celebration Of The MC5*, and followed by a world tour, awkwardly branded DKT/MC5 to remind everyone this was not a reunion. Wayne briefed Dennis and Mike, guitarist Marshall Crenshaw and two lead singers: Mudhoney's Mark Arm and Lemonheads' Evan Dando. Although Wayne would keep the band together for several years, the euphoria of the 100 Club was short-lived: Mike confided to the guitarist that playing with Dennis had lost its appeal and that he was only in it for the bread; Dennis still had no appetite for lassooing his wilder instincts behind the traps; and Dando proved a crotchety co-worker, addicted to garage sales and 'filling the bus up with crap', as Wayne put it. On more serious compulsions, drink and drugs issues saw the vocalist dismissed while the band toured Japan. Several other musicians would be in and out of DKT/MC5's revolving door before Wayne called time in 2011. For 2008's annual Meltdown at the Royal Festival Hall, curators Massive Attack rounded up Kramer, a reconciled Davis and Thompson, John Sinclair, guitarist Adam Pearson, Alice In Chains' vocalist William DuVall and long-time 5 freaks Primal Scream for a memorable concert, the results preserved on an album/DVD entitled, with great originality, *Black To Comm*.

Inspired by a prisoner rehabilitation programme established in the UK by Billy Bragg, Wayne set up Jail Guitar Doors, a non-profit named after an old B-side written about his drug travails by Joe Strummer. He also helped introduce creative music and songwriting therapy to inmates of correctional institutions across the US. Speaking to Jim Kerr in 2018, he deplored how an American prison population of 350,000 had ballooned to 2.3 million in the forty years since his own incarceration:

I don't believe it's going to help any of them. Prison is a medieval concept. I believe in the rule of law, in safe streets and being held accountable if you break the social contract. But I think the punishment should fit the crime, and that's the last thing we do in this country.

In 2018, Wayne published an acclaimed and abrasively candid memoir, *The Hard Stuff*. That May, he once again remade/remodelled MC5 for an anniversary tour. With Rob, Sonic and Mike sadly departed and Machine Gun then indisposed, he instructed vocalist/harpist Marcus Durant (Zen Guerrilla), guitarist Kim Thayil and drummer Matt Cameron (Soundgarden), drummer Brendan Canty (Fugazi) and bassists Billy Gould (Faith No More) and Doug Pinnick (King's X) to help refashion as much of the old MC5 zest and unrest as one grizzled Boomer and several relatively fresh-faced GenXs could manage. (The live evidence, comprising mainly 5 classics, can be heard as Disc 2 of a limited release of the band's final MC5-attributed album, *Heavy Lifting*.) While the MC50 tour was another commercial lemon, the MC5 mini-mes were critically acclaimed, and enthusiasm grew for the original band. Several decades after Lester Bangs, pundits who had dissed the 5 as mere Whoalikes suddenly experienced their own Damascene conversion, while many a grey eminence insisted they'd always said MC5 were the true punk progenitors. From poseurs, plagiarists and pariahs, suddenly MC5 was the name to drop in impolite society.

On 2 February 2024, following several years of philanthropy and genuinely positive activism, Wayne succumbed to pancreatic cancer at a Los Angeles hospital at the age of 75. By May and the loss of Dennis Thompson, bookending John Sinclair's fatal heart attack in April at 82, the last two men standing from the classic MC5 lineup had passed.

A definitive and much-admired history, *MC5: An Oral Biography Of Rock's Most Revolutionary Band*, by Ben Edmonds, Brad Tolinski and Jaan Uhelszki, was published on 8 October, nine days before The Man finally ensnared MC5 within the Rock and Roll Hall of Fame. William DuVall told the BBC: 'It's just so wrong. They're finally getting into the Hall of Fame just in time for none of them to be here.' 2024 also saw the release of the first long-player since *High Time*. It was the last to be accredited to MC5.

Heavy Lifting (2024)

Personnel:
Wayne Kramer: guitar, vocal, bass, keyboards
Brad Brooks: vocal, keyboards, harmonica
Don Was: bass
Vicki Randle: vocal, bass, percussion
Abe Laboriel, Jr: drums
Winston A. Watson, Jr: drums
Stevie Salas: guitar
Special guests:
Dennis Thompson: drums
William DuVall: vocal
Bob Ezrin: vocal
Tim McIlrath: vocal
Tom Morello: guitar
Vernon Reid: guitar
Slash: guitar
Joe Berry: tenor sax
Produced & engineered: Bob Ezrin
Recorded at The Waystation; Dr. Bronner's All-One; Industrial Amusement
Recordings; Shabby Road (all Los Angeles)
Released: 18 October 2024
Highest chart position: (US Billboard 200) 54; (UK Official Albums Chart) 77

This sounds to me like an MC5 record.
Bob Ezrin

The posthumous *Heavy Lifting*, on which Kramer began work during the Covid-19 pandemic, should have been his eighth solo. This reckoned without the persuasive efforts of a certain fêted producer. Four years before, Wayne had reconnected with his old Motor City pal Alice Cooper, who needed guitar for a new album, *Detroit Stories*.

At the desk was Bob Ezrin, who'd produced most of Alice's previous records and had worked for such rock paragons as Pink Floyd, Lou Reed and Deep Purple.

Wayne asked Bob to appraise some music he'd written with Brad Brooks, a singer-songwriter based in San Francisco. As Ezrin recounted to *Classic Rock* in 2024:

Of course I said yes. [Wayne] explained it was going to be the soundtrack for a film that he was writing called Heavy Lifting, about a heist. It didn't sound like the music for a heist movie. What I really heard in it was a spirit of rebellion, challenging social norms and staring down American values.

Kramer was sceptical. 'There are almost none of us left any more,' observed the guitarist. 'But there's you,' Bob reminded him, adding a pithy throwout that would give its name to a 2022 tour and was even nearly a record title: 'We are all MC5.'

Having come around to Ezrin's fancy of creating an MC5 album *de nos jours*, Kramer enlisted Brooks to help add new songs to the tracklist. Belated and renewed interest in the 5, and the recent MC50 and DKT/MC5 outings, seemed reason enough to eschew the leader's name in the credits for that of the classic band. But the 5 of *Heavy Lifting* remains less a homogeneous group than a collection of discrete individuals yoked to a unifying idea. Far from a stable mothership of vocalist, two guitarists, bassist and drummer orbited by star guests, 'MC5' as flagged on the sleeve speaks to the inclusivity suggested by Ezrin's *leitmotif*: we are all a pick'n'mix assortment, all first among equals, of radical soulmates, funk-metal warriors and go-to session stalwarts.

The MC5 sobriquet bound the hirelings into an ever-rotating extended family. Among those spread across four LA studios were DuVall, Slash (Guns N' Roses/Velvet Revolver), Vernon Reid (Living Colour), Tom Morello (Rage Against The Machine, a latterday outrider of MC5's Republican Guard if ever there was one), bassist Don Was and – the icing on the hash cookie for any 5 fan – a rejuvenated Dennis Thompson. Yet despite the Machine Gun hammering away on two tracks and Ezrin's starry-eyed ambitions for the album as a whole, 'We Are All MC5' really turned out to be We Are All Wayne Kramer and heavy friends.

It would be harsh indeed to dismiss the titular MC5 of *Heavy Lifting* as a cynical exercise in marketing. And it feels churlish to issue anything other than a rave review of such a well-meaning record. Long grown out of the dope and disorder of his youth, Wayne is too essentially decent, as man and musician. To be fair, the album rocks out pleasantly under Ezrin's judicious eye and, other than some rerouting into musical territory hitherto wisely uncharted by MC5, tries hard to recreate the restless insubordination of the band in their pomp. But ultimately *Heavy Lifting* is a journeyman exercise in modern, generic hard rock/funk, and too many times removed from what it really wants to be: the completist fourth quarter of a brief but extraordinary body of work. For any MC5 fundi, even any rock 'n' roll fan who's been around as many blocks as the band, *Kick Out The Jams*, *Back In The USA* and *High Time*, plus a few singles, carefully chosen retrospectives and live boots, remain the gold standard: the only ones lurking with intent to bitch-slap you back to the Motor City, with extreme prejudice, long after the remoulds have worn away.

'Heavy Lifting' 3.20 (Wayne Kramer, Brad Brooks)
Kramer's nod to Rage Against The Machine. Guitarist/singer Tom Morello sets his vocal to rapid automatic fire, loosely apeing the restless drive of his own

LA rap-metallurgists without straying too far from his current brief. The bonecrunching riff, written by Morello and reminiscent of Rainbow's power anthem 'Stargazer', fuels the lyrical conceit to Wayne's eponymous, unrealised crime-caper movie, in which a failed screenwriter-stroke-villain has the moxie, guns and 'ceps to make off with an armoured car. In a song as stuffed with outlaw chic as the Baader-Meinhof complex, 'good drugs at my hand', it's easy to imagine the cool co-conspirators planning the heist and loading the Uzis.

'Barbarians At The Gate' 4.18 (Kramer, Brooks)
In August 1968, as the US prepared to choose its thirty-seventh president, MC5 played for the thousands of antiwar protesters who gathered in Chicago for the Democratic National Convention. Fifty-three years later, another pitchfork army, their rage stoked by an even angrier forty-fifth president, breached the portals of Washington DC's Capitol Building, bringing the Constitution and the Union closer to the precipice than even John Sinclair could have imagined. Again more Wayne Kramer solo than MC5, the song is suitably punchy, with great guitar from Kramer and gobiron harp from Brooks. No prizes for guessing which 'barbarians' Wayne and Brad are thinking of here, although it should be remembered that no deaths were recorded when the Class of '68 convened at the DNC, neither did anyone claim that Richard Nixon stole the election from Pigasus.

'Change, No Change' 4.03 (Kramer, Brooks)
As Brad Brooks told Robert Pally in a 2025 interview, '[Kramer and I] were writing about the world that was going insane during Covid.' Sung by Brooks, 'Change, No Change' zeroes in on the pandemic plight of the homeless in Oakland, CA. The outcome is worthy by sentiment – Brad's well-crafted words speak to a community's defiance as 'Culprits and hypocrites take their oath' while 'Corporates and delegates aim the scope' – but sluggish by nature, never really taking flight after the assault and battery of Abe Laboriel Jr's opening drum salvo.

'The Edge Of The Switchblade' 4.16 (Kramer)
Originally recorded by Wayne for his 1995 solo album *The Hard Stuff*, he adds little to that record's best track. This hard-rocking song lyrically celebrates MC5, referencing the Chicago DNC and how his old band was renegade, outside the mainstream, the true cutting edge of the switchblade. It's pumped with the kind of lover-poet-warrior machismo that sometimes strutted around Rob Tyner's lyrics, not to mention Slash's suitably lacerating guitar.

'Black Boots' 2:53 (Tim McIlrath)
Tim McIlrath, of the Chicago punk band Rise Against, hands back the mic to Brooks on a song whose gut-thumping riff suggests 'Black Boots' walked in

on the same session that produced the album's title track. Where 'Heavy Lifting' was an escapist fantasy – part film treatment, part gangster pipe-dream – this is a paranoid premonition of war, illustrating the helplessness of the average grunt which the issue of regulation footwear and a SIG Sauer can only, paradoxically, reinforce. 'Black Boots' is what happens 'when our eyes won't close' and 'when the air runs out', and it's the blackest song on the album.

'I Am The Fun (The Phoney)' 3.35 (Kramer, Brooks)
Although Brooks' young family whoop and holler over the opening bars – the singer later described the track as his favourite on the record – the fun has a definite phoney edge. Brad told Pally that while the life-&-soul character swanning around the lyric is disagreeably self-confident, '[He] also has this tiny bit of self-awareness that maybe [he's] full of shit but no one seems to care ... It's also a very LA party-crasher entitlement rock-star thing with the lyric: I could destroy everything in this room.' Inspired by the funk into which he and Kramer were being absorbed as if it were musical tofu – of which more below – the sour words and even more acidic lead guitar are let down by Brooks' alkaline vocal and a vanilla groove that never properly takes off.

'Twenty-Five Miles' 3.53 (Johnny Bristol, Harvey Fuqua, Edwin Starr)
This is better, an exuberant, horn-driven reading of Edwin Starr's 1968 hit. Who'd have thought, way back when, that Wayne Kramer, lead guitarist of MC5, would one day be retreading a classic of the Northern Soul dancefloor? Keep the faith. It's great. 'Nuff said.

'Because Of Your Car' 3.02 (Kramer, Brooks)
The chorus refrain mines a similar seam to the notorious 'Free Love Freeway' by Ricky Gervaise's comic grotesque, David Brent. Since its first airing in *The Office* in 2001, the US open-road parody has taken on a strangely ironic cachet, licensed for advertising and raved about as if it were a postmodern 'Take It Easy'. While the song was very funny in its original context, why Kramer and Brooks felt the need to disinter its remains here is a mystery. The thumpingly moody riff just about saves the song, although the high-register vocal (not to mention the ghost of Brent) feels out of place on an album that sometimes can't decide whether it's punk, funk or sitcom soundtrack.

'Boys Who Play With Matches' 3.10 (Kramer, Brooks)
Released as a single in August 2024, with a slashing rhythm guitar cut loose from the same Stones' *Sticky Fingers* session that produced 'Can't You Hear Me Knocking'. The boys in question, who with 'firebombs and lethal dispatches ... gotta burn the golden rule', could be any insufferably loud rock 'n' roll band with a penchant for disruption. Remind you of anyone?

'Blind Eye' 3.16 (Kramer, Brooks, Bob Ezrin, Jill Sobule)
Despite an album-wide disconnect between punk and funk, there's still room for a truly great pop song. The first of two tracks on *Heavy Lifting* graced by Dennis Thompson, 'Blind Eye' rattles along on an exhilaratingly motorvating bassline and has a chorus hook like a grappling iron. Although the whole thing suggests an irresistible single, the lyrics tell of how comfort and 'a perfect life' spawn blindness and apathy. 'When I sign in it goes away,' sings Brooks, the world of hits and video games providing refuge from news images often far from optimistic.

'Can't Be Found' 3.48 (Kramer, Brooks)
How The Rolling Stones might have sounded if (a) they'd taken a pass on Ronnie Wood in 1975 in favour of Mick Ronson, and (b) the Glimmer Twins had managed to resist the era's blandishments of funky musical settings the Stones were rarely comfortable with. Here the shredding axe belongs to Vernon Reid, one of the finest guitarists of his generation, who steps up alongside Machine Gun for the album's most honest and unpretentious track. Swaggering and life-affirming, 'it's a song that makes you wanna drive faster, which is very Detroit,' as Brad Brooks told Pally. 'Nothing left to do except to dance and sing as it's burning down,' he continues, from the vantage point of a writer who knows 'everything's fucked up' but must still 'continue and … decipher what is the truth.'

'Blessed Release' 3.03 (Kramer, Brooks)
'It was really fun and so different.' Despite singer Brooks' enthusiasm – and, it must be said, Wayne's early unconditional love of James Brown – funk was no more credible in the hands of MC5 than it was the Stones. The brilliance of Watts and Wyman notwithstanding, 'staying on the one' was always best left to rhythm geniuses such as Brown, Sly and Parliament/Funkadelic, whom Brooks cited as influences when he and Kramer put together 'this stream of consciousness dance song'. As it labours with the falsetto vocal stylings of Mick Jagger in the dark days of *Black And Blue*, 'Blessed Release' is unredeemed even when the band fall into an avant-punk coda, as if they've belatedly remembered that We Are All MC5 and not The Ohio Players.

'Hit It Hard' 2.42 (Kramer, Brooks)
From a bang to a whimper. If *Heavy Lifting*'s title track kickstarted the album like Thomas 'Hitman' Hearns in a championship bout, by the end 'Hit It Hard' does its best to live down to its name. Joe Berry's squally tenor sax tries to lift an out-of-sync funk workout that calls to mind Bowie's 'Fame'. It's a low-juice finale that speaks to Wayne's old contention that the band often shot their load too soon, with nothing substantive at the death. Just as a drifting 'Starship' left the end of side two of *Kick Out The Jams* lost in space, there's a strange, sad symmetry in repeating the anticlimax here, on the final album.

The Legacy

Plenty of water has flowed beneath the Gordie Howe Bridge since the original MC5 were visiting structural vandalism on an innocent old Detroit ballroom. *Kick Out The Jams* sounded radically new in 1969, while *Back In The USA* and *High Time* proved the 5 were unafraid to scuttle the subsequent expectations of record executives, critics and fans – even if some deviations were not so much planned as serendipitous or ill-fated. Since then, MC5 – their toughest of senior coalition partners, The Who, paternally and metaphorically watching their backs – have nudged dozens of hard rock, punk, grunge, metal and nu-metal bands into cranking that shit up and seeing just how far they can push the limiters. The passing years and improving studio technology – not to mention a socio-political environment so accustomed to hard rock's unedifying habits AC/DC get played in Tesco and a Birmingham bridge is named after Black Sabbath – have knocked out the lumps, bumps and blemishes, the music more ruthlessly machined with the arrival of every youth tribe, sub-genre and new release of Pro Tools.

Despite the best efforts of Jon Landau, and sometimes even the band's own leader, MC5 were never about flawlessness. They were creatively and aesthetically imperfect, and both product and symptom of their time. Just as no V8 Mustang cantered away from Ford's 1967 line preconfigured with WiFi and SatNav, the analogue torment of five layabouts out of a smokestack city in its death throes would hardly convince if it had been generated on a £500 laptop loaded with Auto-Tune.

Meantime, how fared the struggle? On the White Panthers' ten commandments, MC5 were at best cautiously agnostic, if not downright atheist. Neither was their province howling protest aimed at the violent overthrow of the state. True, it was close, and many juries remain out. Michael Davis and Dennis Thompson insisted they'd enlisted only for kicks and chicks, while Wayne Kramer, Fred Smith and Rob Tyner were ambivalent. But MC5 were the sound and fury of the revolution, not the substance. On their most confrontational record – the debut live set John Sinclair hoped would be a declaration of war – the one song whose sentiments could be described as political was a non-original, modified for fashionable agitprop topicality but hardly a rallying cry.

Social comment and subversive exhortations had crept into the lyrics by the third album, but I'd ask the jury to test concurrent 'underground' evidence presented by The Fugs, David Peel, Jefferson Airplane, The Doors, Country Joe McDonald and CSNY; and, in Britain, by Mick Farren's Deviants, Edgar Broughton, Pete Brown, Roy Harper and even The Rolling Stones, at a time when the Street Fighting Man was more likely to heed the teachings of The Little Red Book than The Telegraph Tax Guide. By the prevailing standards established by those and other artists, the fresh wind blowing against the empire was not coming from MC5, who inevitably defaulted to Panthers' Clause 2 whenever anyone mentioned revolution.

In August 2023, Kramer discussed with *Ultimate Guitar* his iconic 'stars & stripes' Stratocaster, of which a decade earlier Fender manufactured six hundred WK signature copies. Wayne told Justin Beckner of his native pride and patriotism, instincts that persisted even at the height of MC5's notoriety:

I decided to have my guitar painted with that motif, the idea behind that was, it's my flag too. It's not just the right-wing flag. In my coming-of-age years, that was the Vietnam War period. The hawks tried to co-opt the symbol of the flag. And I said, 'Hey, not so fast. This is my flag, too. And I disagree with this war. I don't support this war and it's my patriotic duty to say, I don't agree with what the government is doing. Democracy requires participation. So I've just continued with using that symbol to represent the fact that we live in a pluralistic culture with differing views and differing ideas. It's messy sometimes, but it's the symbol of the American experiment, which I support. I don't think it's the greatest system in the world. But it beats the pants off of whatever is second.

In the few years since Wayne was articulating values that some still believe conflicted with MC5's own, and the five decades and counting since John Sinclair attempted to channel rebellion through five working-class, all-American boys, societal change has been seismic. Throughout the world, common moral principles have declined; in their place, an apparently unstoppable populism, annulling the collectivist ideals of 1960s' counterculture even while cherrypicking the same milieu's quest for total freedom. If Sinclair's WPP manifesto once was a naïvely idealistic blueprint for the dismantling of capitalism, for today's libertarian tech bros it's a user's guide to doing whatever they damn well please. Having taken the downpayment, it seems the dodgy totalitarian building firm have almost finished the job.

So the revolution wasn't about to be televised from MC5's wheelhouse. But to what extent were they 'punk'? Wayne saw the term as less an explicitly socio-musical tribe than an oblique way of doing what comes naturally: 'Beethoven, Charlie Parker, John Coltrane, all those guys were punks in the sense that they had to reinvent music for their generations,' he told Ryan Place of *Detroit Bookfest* in 2018. If the guitarist finally accepted that MC5 were themselves reinventors and punk's standard-bearers, following through by tacitly convincing everyone else to think the same, he was at first unimpressed by the British Class of '76. Wayne did not personally identify as a punk, and with very good reason.

While in prison, not long after Pistols-in-waiting Steve Jones and Paul Cook were quietly relieving the Hammersmith Odeon of David Bowie's PA system, Wayne read a *Billboard* article extolling MC5 as a signal influence on The Ramones and other punkische New York groups. As Alexis Petridis reported after interviewing Wayne for the *Guardian* in 2024, any jailbird explicitly styling himself a punk was courting disaster:

Kramer was so horrified, he tore the magazine up and flushed it down the nearest toilet. As he put it, 'from where I was sat, 'punk' did not have a good ring to it. In jail, a punk is somebody that they knock down and make their girlfriend. You know: 'I'm gonna make you my punk'. That kind of talk could get you killed, right?

If self-preservation once obliged Wayne to disown allegations of punk, despite MC5's deferred ownership of the genre, his modesty would sweep aside the burden of nominal leadership. But with a convenient label assigned to every 'new' musical idiom, rock's taxonomy becomes ever more confusing and generationally fluid. For music lovers weaned on Bo Diddley, James Brown, Sly Stone and Otis Redding, accusing Mariah Carey and J-Lo of R&B is a stretch too far. If Paul Weller really is the Modfather, where does that leave Roger Daltrey, Ray Davies, Steve Marriott and Rod Stewart? And I've lost count of my own pub-bore admonitions that The Count Five were a punk group more than a decade before The Clash.

The relevance of such arbitrary pigeonholing to anyone other than journalists, marketing executives and record-store shelf-stackers is questionable. But hang the classifications – just call MC5 what you will: proto-punk, revolutionary rock, heavy metal, jazz-rock fusion from hell, man's inhumanity to man: MC5 were quite simply one of the greatest of all *rock 'n' roll* bands, along with everything, good and bad, attending that catch-all generalisation. And their legacy lives on.

As well as the Pistols and The Clash, among MC5's English beneficiaries were Britpunk's first and finest, The Damned, who tore through a superb 'Looking At You' on *Machine Gun Etiquette* and who, like the 5, were always far from the peri-urban maladroits implied by their early public image. 'Kick Out The Jams' has been covered by everyone and his motherfucker, from Blue Öyster Cult to Afrika Bambaataa, Jeff Buckley to duetting Detroiters Suzi Quatro and Alice Cooper. Among the many doffing their caps to the group that did more than most to give them life are Black Flag, The Cult, Faith No More, Fugazi, King's X, Metallica, The Minutemen, Motörhead, Pearl Jam, Primal Scream, Rage Against The Machine, Soundgarden and the Motor City's own White Stripes. In 1975, even Lou Reed got in on the act – not that the former Velvets capo would likely have admitted it – with his stupefying, 64-minute rejection of rhythm, melody, structure and record company expectations, *Metal Machine Music*. MC5's influence pops up unexpectedly, too: were they in Neil Young's crosshairs when, with Crazy Horse, the grungemeister bred the huge, overdriven, teeth-scraping codas in live performance captured on *Weld*, or the deafening *musique concrète* of that album's companion volume, *Arc*?

It would be good to think that all these and more occasionally gaze respectfully up – or down? – at MC5, pondering where life, the music and everything would have taken them without five scuzzy 1968 Detroit factory rats inexplicably entrusted with recording contracts and electricity. And surely Wayne, Rob, Sonic, Mike and Machine Gun are all glowering down – or up? – with eternally teenage contempt, showing no respect whatsoever as they holler, at any volume the customer wants as long as it's loud:

KICK OUT THE JAMS, MOTHERFUCKERS!